Abiding in Christ

*Meditations on the Lord's Prayer,
the Sermon on the Mount,
and the Ten Commandments*

Reginald Hollis

Anselm Press

Abiding in Christ

1994
Anselm Press

Copyright © by Reginald Hollis

Abiding in Christ was previously published in 1987 by Anglican Book Center, Toronto

This edition printed and bound in the United States

ISBN 0-9642201-0-5

Contents

Introduction 7

The Lord's Prayer 9
The Sermon on the Mount 29
The Ten Commandments 59

To Marcia,
my wife
and prayer partner

One of the most powerful invitations Jesus gives is that we should abide, or remain, in him. He uses the metaphor of a vine and points out "no branch can bear fruit by itself; it must remain in the vine" (John 15:4). In the same way, there cannot be an unconnected Christian, and Jesus points out "neither can you bear fruit unless you remain in me" (John 15:4).

The very essence of living the Christian life, of being a Christian, is our relationship with Jesus. We are to be related to him as integrally as a branch is connected to a tree. We are part of him in the way that a hand or foot is part of a body. We are built into him the way one brick is mortared to another and the whole building held together with the foundation and key stone. These different metaphors are all in the New Testament. In their own way, Jesus, Paul, and Peter insist on the reality of and necessity for our relationship with Christ. This relationship with Christ inevitably involves our relationship with others who are "in him." As we cannot be isolated from Jesus, so we cannot be isolated from our brothers and sisters in him.

In this series of meditations on the Lord's Prayer, the Sermon on the Mount, and the Ten Commandments, we are looking at the two themes of our relationship with him and our relationship with one another. The prayer which begins with our relationship with "our Father" and his will, ends with our forgiveness of one another. In any case, it is clear from the beginning that it is "our Father" and not "my Father." True prayer can never grow out of a religion of individualism.

The Sermon on the Mount is a call to the life which grows out of a relationship with Jesus. It calls for complete integrity in our response to God. The sermon, however, is not about heroic living emanating from personal inner resources. It is about a life based on the firm foundation of Jesus Christ.

To include the Ten Commandments in a book about abiding in Christ may at first sound strange. The commandments are the old law, the ethic of the Old Testament. Although the "new law" of the Sermon on the Mount takes us further, the old foundation still stands. Again the dual relation to God and neighbour is clear. The first four commandments speak of a relationship with the one God who is our creator. The other six deal with relationship with parents and neighbours and the whole business of living together in society. Jesus summed up the commandments: "Love the Lord your God with all your heart and with all your soul and with all your mind and with all your strength . . . Love your neighbour as yourself" (Mark 12:30–31). Since he concluded, "There is no commandment greater than these," they can be regarded as foundation thinking in our consideration of abiding in Christ.

Many have written about the Lord's Prayer, the Sermon on the Mount, and the Ten Commandments. In many churches these passages were stencilled on the chancel walls as words to lead to meditation on the deeper things of God. Anyone who meditates on these central passages of Scripture finds new insights into our calling to abide in Christ and to live for Christ. The meditations in this book are not meant to replace individual meditation, but to stimulate more personal reflection on the word of God.

I have not hesitated to quote liberally from Scripture. The Bible is not to be interpreted by verses in isolation. Rather, Scripture must be interpreted by Scripture. One part of the Bible casts light on another part. The more we soak ourselves in the Scripture, the more we shall be acquainted with the mind of the Lord and the more we shall be enabled to abide in Christ.

Meditations on Scripture should lead us to prayer. The prayers at the end of each meditation are not blank verse. They are set out in line form to mark out separate thoughts. The prayers collect up the thoughts of the meditations, but they are not offered primarily as prayers to be used. Just as the meditations are meant to stimulate personal meditation, so the purpose of the prayers is to lead each individual to pray.

By praying, we open ourselves to the life-giving sap of the vine. Meditation and prayer help us to abide in him. The test of that reality is not the fervour of our feelings in prayer. Abiding in the vine is about bearing fruit. Abiding in Christ means bearing the fruit of the Spirit — love, joy, and peace. Jesus said, "You did not choose me, but I chose you to go and bear fruit — fruit that will last" (John 15:16).

*The
Lord's
Prayer*

It was after he had been praying one day that the disciples asked Jesus, "Lord teach us to pray," and he said to them, "When you pray say, 'Our Father, who art in in heaven, hallowed be thy name . . .'" That prayer which we use so frequently is the prayer that he gave us; it is the *Lord's* Prayer. It arose out of his prayers, and as we continue to use it we pray with him.

Our prayers lack the dedication to the Father's will that characterizes our Lord's prayers. We come often with wandering minds, with sinful lives, and with the lack of a deep intention. In the weakness of our praying, we know that our prayers have real meaning because they are in the context of his prayers. We pray because he prayed. More significantly, we pray because he prays. The value of my prayer is not that I have become "a good pray-er." The value of my prayer is that I come to God in Jesus Christ, in the context of his offering of himself to God in his prayers, in his earthly life, in his death, and in his resurrection life.

Praying is not simply something *I* do. God takes the initiative in drawing me to himself so that I want to reach out to him. The Lord Jesus prays for me, for "he is able to save completely those who come to God through him, because he always lives to intercede for them" (Hebrews 7:25). God the Holy Spirit is engaged in prayer for me, for St Paul writes, "the Spirit intercedes for the saints in accordance with God's will" (Romans 8:27).

If you have some problems in praying, you're not the first! Even St Paul says, "We do not know what we ought to pray" (Romans 8:26), and the Lord's disciples fell asleep while they were praying. It's not surprising that we are weak pray-ers. All our lives we will have problems praying. The important thing is that we have the intention to go on praying. In our weakness, in our wandering thoughts, in our sinful lives, we must keep coming back to set aside a time consciously to open our lives to God.

We do need to *work* at our praying, but our praying will be off balance as long as we think the essence of our praying is what *we* do. Prayer is what we let him do in us and though us. Unless we abide in Christ, our prayer is worth nothing.

O Lord,
I too often think
that it's *my* prayer,
that *I* make the effort
and set aside the time.
But even when I pray my best
there's an inherent weakness,
for "we do not know how to pray as we ought."
Help me to know that
my prayer has value
because it's in the context of your prayer,
because your Spirit continually intercedes for me.
Help me to pray
with persistence and faith.
Help me to grow in the art of praying,
but, above all, help me
to know that my prayer
is real only
when I abide in Christ.

Our Father, who art in Heaven

To Jesus, God was the Father. His prayers began, "Father . . ."
We don't have many of Jesus' prayers recorded, but in Matthew
11:25 his prayer begins, "I praise you, Father, Lord of heaven
and earth, because you have hidden these things from the wise
and learned, and revealed them to little children. Yes, Father, for
this was your good pleasure." In John 11:41 his prayer begins,
"Father, I thank you that you have heard me." In Matthew 26:39
he begins, "My Father, if it is possible, may this cup be taken
from me. Yet not as I will, but as you will." On the cross he
prayed, "Father, forgive them, for they do not know what they
are doing" (Luke 23:34). And his final earthly prayer was "Father,
into your hands I commit my spirit" (Luke 23:46).

The Lord himself calls God "Father," and he teaches us to call God "Father." "When you pray," he says to his disciples, "say, 'Our Father.'" For us it is not *my* Father, but *our* Father because of our community with him. With Jesus we say, "Our Father." We can call God our Father because Jesus has become our brother. "Jesus is not ashamed to call them brothers," says the letter to the Hebrews (Hebrews 2:11), and St Paul describes Jesus as "the firstborn among many brothers" (Romans 8:29).

But it is not merely a fraternal association with Jesus as our brother that enables us to call God "Father." The only reason that we can call God "Father" is that we are "in Jesus." Because we are "in him and he in us," we make our prayer in Jesus' name. "In Jesus' name" is not some magical formula we add to our prayers. Rather, we come to God in Jesus. We do not plead our righteousness, what we have done, how good we are at praying, but we come to God only because of what Jesus has done and is doing for us.

Unless we are aware that we come to the Father in Jesus, we so easily become like another son who in Jesus' parable came to his father and said, "Father, give me my share of the estate" (Luke 15:12). The prodigal son wanted his share of the inheritance, he wanted immediately that to which he felt he had a legal right. So often we come to God demanding our rights. We think it our right that someone we love should be healed, that things go our way, that what we want we should get. It's not just a selfish demand; we compare ourselves with other people and demand our rights. If someone else's mother can live until 80, why must my mother die at 46? If someone else can get a certain position, why must I stay where I am? If someone else enjoys good health, why should I have a heart attack? If someone else has an attractive home, don't I have the same right?

The prodigal son had to come to the point where he was willing to say, "Father, I have sinned against heaven and against you. I am no longer worthy to be called your son" (Luke 15:21). It's only when we get to that stage in our praying that we find the reality of prayer. But despite the fact that we have sinned, that we are not worthy to be called his son or daughter, we can come to the Father in Jesus. Jesus is the declaration of our forgiveness. In Jesus we are made clean. In Jesus we are made worthy to be called the Father's children. As we pray at the eucharist, "We are not worthy so much as to gather up the crumbs under thy table. But thou art the same Lord, whose property is always to have mercy." No wonder that prayer concludes with the petition, "that we may evermore dwell in him, and he in us."

O Lord,
I have too often come to you in prayer
demanding my rights.
I never say it that way,
but you know and I know
what I mean:
I want my rightful share.
You are my Father,
but I have the right of inheritance
only because Jesus died for me.
He became my brother
so that I could call you "our Father."
May I come to you
in the right that's only mine because
I abide in Christ.

Hallowed be thy name

God appeared to Moses at Horeb. He appeared in the burning bush that wasn't consumed. His purpose was to send Moses back into Egypt to bring the people out of their slavery. Moses said to God, "Suppose I go to the Israelites and say to them, 'The God of your fathers has sent me to you,' and they ask me, 'What is his name?' Then what shall I tell them?" God said to Moses, "I am who I am. This is what you are to say to the Israelites: 'I AM has sent me to you'" (Exodus 3:13–14).

God is not encompassed by a name. No name is great enough to characterize him. He is the ground of being; he is beyond our comprehension. We may have begun this prayer calling him our

Father, but we must recognize that we do not comprehend him, we do not control him. We call him the familial "our Father," but that's no cause for being familiar with him. Indeed, we do well to recognize that it is only by the Holy Spirit we can call him Father. St Paul writes, "By him we cry, 'Abba, Father.' The Spirit himself testifies with our spirit that we are God's children" (Romans 8:15-16).

Some ancient peoples used to think that when they knew the name of a god, they then had some special power over the god. It was a kind of secret knowledge that enabled you to get what you wanted. For the Christian, though, there is a very clear awareness that we cannot manipulate God. Prayer is not manipulation. Prayer, rather, is awe and wonder before the great mystery of God. With reverence and fear we sing, "Holy, holy, holy, Lord God of hosts. Heaven and earth are full of thy glory. Glory be to thee, O Lord most high."

God's greatness is unfathomable, and we would be lost before it if God had not taken the initiative in speaking to us in his Son. St Paul writes, "For God, who said, 'Let light shine out of darkness,' made his light shine in our hearts to give us the light of the knowledge of the glory of God in the face of Christ" (2 Corinthians 4:6).

It is in Jesus Christ that we see in the clearest way the nature of God. In him we see that God is love. We see the self-emptying love that took the form of a servant and became obedient unto death, even death on a cross. "Therefore," says St Paul, "God exalted him to the highest place and gave him the name that is above every name, that at the name of Jesus every knee should bow, in heaven and on earth and under the earth, and every tongue confess that Jesus Christ is Lord, to the glory of God the Father" (Philippians 2:9-11).

It is as we abide in Jesus, as we kneel before him, as we are amazed by the wonder of his love, as we confess the name of Jesus, Saviour, as we adore him, that we shall truly pray, "Hallowed be thy name."

O Lord,
I've sometimes prayed
as though we were equals,

but that's not prayer,
for the truth is that you are
infinitely great
and I am so small,
human, frail, and sinful.
May I stand in awe at your greatness,
but may your Spirit within me
call you Father,
and may I know
the warmth of your love,
as I abide in Christ.

Thy Kingdom come

People see prayer at its lowest level when they think it is
something like a slot machine. You put your request in at the top,
and out at the bottom comes your answer. It's some kind of magic
to get what you want. But the idea of prayer is transformed when
you see it as part of the action of God. When we pray, "Thy
kingdom come," we see prayer in the context of what *God* is
doing. God is bringing in his kingdom, and prayer is aligning
myself with that kingdom. In prayer the emphasis is not on what
I am doing to change the world, but on what God is doing. Prayer
is the *recognition* that God is bringing in his kingdom.

Jesus taught us that the kingdom is not far away in the future,
but is here now. He said, "If I drive out demons by the finger
of God, then the kingdom of God has come to you" (Luke 11:20).
When Jesus was overcoming evil, it was a sign of the presence
of God's kingdom. Jesus said to people, "The kingdom of God
is among you."

Jesus' parables of the kingdom were often ones that demanded
response to God's action. When someone said to him, "Blessed
is the man who will eat at the feast in the kingdom of God" (Luke
14:15), Jesus told of a banquet for which invitations were sent
out: "Come, for everything is now ready." But people began to

make excuses. For Jesus, the kingdom was a present reality, seen in his wonderful healing powers, but people made their excuses for not responding to God's invitation.

God *is* bringing in his kingdom. We may not think it is fast enough in coming. The kingdoms of this world are not yet transformed into the kingdom of our Lord and Christ. But God's timing is not our timing. In the fullness of time he will act decisively. But let us not deceive ourselves and think that he is absent. The greatest sign of his initiative is that sign of his love for us in Jesus' dying for us. That is *the* sign, the assurance of his victory, reaffirmed by his resurrection. No wonder St Paul can sing out, "Thanks be to God! He gives us the victory through our Lord Jesus Christ" (1 Corinthians 15:57).

God is working in so many ways in our lives. He is changing people today. He is advancing the cause of medical research, he is providing healing hands and caring hearts in doctors and nurses, and he is healing through prayer. He is bringing a beauty to human life, a caring quality. But the enemy is still strong, dividing men and causing bitterness to spring up. The enemy motivates the desire to possess more and more, and human life is often counted cheap to acquire political domination. If it weren't for the fact that God is carrying his purpose out, the world would have been finished ages ago. Despite our sin, God still loves the world so much that he gives his only begotten Son. He shares the Spirit, whose harvest is those beautiful qualities that heal human relationships — love, joy, peace, patience, kindness, goodness, faithfulness, humility, and self-control.

To pray abiding in Jesus is to rest in the assurance that God is bringing in his kingdom. It is to put ourselves on his side in the battle against all that would destroy the beauty of human society. It is to respond to his invitation to join in the victory feast.

O Lord,
my prayer seemed too small
until I saw it
as part of the coming of
the kingdom of God.
You are working your work,

the work of the kingdom.
You are always turning water to wine;
you are always healing the sick;
you are always overcoming evil with good;
you are always bringing people to new birth;
you are always raising the dead;
you are working in me, Lord.
I pray for grace
to respond to your invitation,
to share in your work and your kingdom,
and always to abide in Christ.

Thy will be done on earth as it is in heaven

It is easy to say, "Thy will be done," when we really mean deep down, "My will be done." That is not surprising, for the Bible diagnoses that the basic problem of human living is in the assertion, "My will be done." That is what the story of Adam and Eve was about. Eve was tempted to disobey the will of God, "You are free to eat from any tree in the garden; but you must not eat from the tree of the knowledge of good and evil" (Genesis 2:16-17). But when Eve contemplated what the devil told her would be the advantages of eating that fruit, she decided to do what she wanted and not what God wanted, even though the devil's account of the consequences was just the opposite of what God had said, for the Lord had told her that she would die. This story has implications for all mankind. We all want to say to God in so many ways, "My will be done."

In contrast, the mark of Jesus' life was the desire to do the will of the Father. "I have come down from heaven not to do my will but to do the will of him who sent me" (John 6:38), said Jesus. The writer of the letter to the Hebrews points us to Psalm 40 as interpreting the Lord's life, "Then I said, 'Here I am — it is written about me in the scroll — I have come to do your will, O God'"

(Hebrews 10:7). And he goes on to say, "By that will, we have been made holy through the sacrifice of the body of Jesus Christ once for all" (Hebrews 10:10). It was to the point of death that he was willing to do the Father's will. It was in the garden of Gethsemane on the eve of the crucifixion that he prayed, "Father, if you are willing, take this cup from me; yet not my will, but yours be done" (Luke 22:42).

Although we are his followers, we often come to our prayers with an underlying idea that we know what is best. We may pray with our lips, "Thy will be done," but we have a hidden agenda. Like Eve we are persuaded that to have a certain thing will bring happiness. It might be a new job or a new home. The teenage boy thinks he would be blissfully happy if a certain girl paid attention to him. The housewife thinks she would be happy if only she had a certain house. The business person thinks he or she would be happy if only they got a certain position. The circumstances are different, and you alone can apply it to yourself.

So often our motives get mixed up. We can persuade ourselves, "That must be God's will for me!" when really, as so often others can see, we are after our own ends. The prophet Isaiah reminds us, " 'For my thoughts are not your thoughts, neither are your ways my ways,' declares the Lord" (Isaiah 55:8).

Sometimes God's ways are extremely puzzling to us. But as Isaiah again reminds us, "Yet, O Lord, you are our Father. We are the clay, you are the potter; we are all the work of your hand" (Isaiah 64:8).

In our perplexity and in our self-centredness, we need to be praying day by day, "Thy will be done." Because our prayer is so sullied by our desires, we must seek to abide in Jesus and say with him, "Thy will be done." We need to claim the victory in his life as he achieved the will of the Father.

O Lord,
I sometimes genuinely don't know
whether I'm doing your will.
I pray, "Thy will be done"
and I claim that

my will is in line with yours,
but I know that
my own desires are strong.
Give me the clear vision
and the steady determination
that come from
abiding in Christ.

Give us this day our daily bread

One of the most common excuses for lack of prayer is that we do not have time. We are so busy doing all the things that need doing, looking after all the things we worry about. We have to work, we have to eat, we have to go to the store, we have to watch the news, we have to read the paper, we have to get our exercise. There is so much to be done, the days are so short, and time flies by so fast.

These are all excuses, for if we knew the priority of prayer, of relating to the Father's will, the other things would fall into place. That was the teaching of Jesus, and if we want to abide in him, we must know the reality of his words concerning the daily needs of life, "Your heavenly Father knows that you need them. But seek first his kingdom and his righteousness, and all things will be given to you as well" (Matthew 6:32-33). In prayer we can come to God for our daily bread, assured that our heavenly Father knows our needs and cares about us.

I once knew a woman who was sick, and we were all praying for her in the parish. I discovered, though, that she would not pray for herself because she thought that would be selfish. Her motive sounds very commendable, but when you look at the Lord's prayer it is obvious that the Lord taught us to pray for ourselves. What we pray for ourselves must be in the larger context, "Thy will be done on earth as it is in heaven." Yet Jesus did not leave us there but taught us to go on, "Give us this day our daily bread." When we abide in Christ, we know that we can come to our heavenly Father with our daily needs.

Of course, when we pray in Jesus, we pray for our daily bread and not for our daily French pastry! It was the Son of man who taught us to pray, "Give us this day our daily bread," who had no where to lay his head. He did not have all the luxuries of the world, but he had all he really needed. He had learned to see and appreciate the luxuries we take for granted in the beauty of nature. He could see the lilies of the field and knew that "not even Solomon in all his splendour was dressed like one of these" (Matthew 6:29). Our prayer must be in that same context, that is, daily declaring, "How many are your works, O Lord! In wisdom you made them all" (Psalm 104:24).

Also, when we are in him we pray, "Give *us*," and not just, "Give *me*." We are part of his body, his family, and we pray for the other members. Prayer is not a way of getting my share, but of offering our common needs to God. We see in St Paul's letters that prayer was the cement for the building blocks of relationship between Paul and his fellow-believers. Each letter begins with the assurance of his prayers for the community to which he is writing. Frequently he asks for their prayers. When we pray for our daily bread, when we pray for each other, we are expressing the reality that together we are in Christ. Being in Christ implies such daily caring for one another, where "If one part suffers, every part suffers with it" (1 Corinthians 12:26). Being in Christ implies such caring for one another, where we offer the whole body to the Father, praying, "Give us this day our daily bread."

O Lord,
I see now that
praying is a way of living.
To pray is
not to be anxious about things,
but to know that my heavenly Father
knows all my needs.
To pray is

to bring all things about which I'm concerned
before you,
knowing that you know my needs
before I ask.
Give me that confidence in prayer
that comes when I trustfully
abide in Christ.

---

*Forgive us our trespasses as we forgive them that trespass
against us.*

Human relationships fall apart when we sin against one another.
Think of it in very personal terms. If I tell a lie to my wife, the
basis of trust between us is weakened. She may not know it is
a lie, but I know, and that knowledge adds a little uneasiness
to our relationship. I have a fear that she might find out. If I had
a secret affair with another woman, I have no doubt that it would
alter the relationship I have with my wife. Our expression of love
and my commitment "to keep me only unto her till death do us
part" would be broken.

In so many ways you can see that when we break the basic commandments against one another our relationships too are broken.
What is true on the level of our human relationships is also true
in our relationship with God. Broken commandments mean
broken relationships. When we come to prayer, we inevitably
come with broken commandments as a part of our lives. St John
says, "If we claim to be without sin, we deceive ourselves and
the truth is not in us" (1 John 1:8).

In my relationship with my wife, I might think she would not
know about my lie or my act of adultery. I could be deceiving
myself. She might know more than I think. But with God I can
be sure that I cannot hide anything in my life from his eyes. The
psalmist says, "Where can I flee from your presence? If I go up
to the heavens, you are there; if I make my bed in the depths,

you are there. If I rise on the wings of the dawn, if I settle on the far side of the sea, even there your hand will guide me, your right hand will hold me fast" (Psalm 139:7b–10). God is one unto whom, as the ancient prayer puts it, "all hearts are open, all desires known, and from whom no secrets are hid." Again the psalm puts it so clearly, "O Lord, you have searched me and you know me. You know when I sit and when I rise; you perceive my thoughts from afar. You discern my going out and my lying down; you are familiar with all my ways. Before a word is on my tongue you know it completely, O Lord" (Psalm 139:1–4).

We can forget his omniscience. We ask, "Will God see?" But our forgetting does not alter the reality. We stand before God as we are, and one of the Bible writers says that before him "all our righteous acts are like filthy rags" (Isaiah 64:6). No wonder St Paul speaks of our putting on Christ as a garment. He writes to the Galatians, "For all of you who were baptized into Christ have clothed yourselves with Christ" (Galatians 3:27).

To stand before God we need to put on Christ, to put on his nature, to put on his righteousness. We are accepted by God not because of the good score we have marked up, but because of the righteousness of Jesus Christ. St Paul knew this clearly. He writes to the Philippians that all the old things in which he used to put his trust were really garbage. They did not add up to much at all because, as he knew, sin ran through them. However, Paul's aim was to "be found in him, not having a righteousness of my own that comes from the law, but that which is through faith in Christ — the righteousness that comes from God and is by faith" (Philippians 3:9).

If our relationship with God is to be open, if our prayer is to be real, an essential element of our prayer must be the request for forgiveness. We make that request in Christ, because we know that in him we are forgiven. Of course, if we are in him, we must try to live as he lived, and one great mark of his life was forgiveness for others. Even as he was dying, his prayer was, "Father, forgive them, for they do not know what they are doing" (Luke 23:34). So we pray, "Forgive us our trespasses as we forgive them that trespass against us."

O Lord,
how do I think
I can come to you
with words
when my life
is not right with you?
Forgive me, Lord,
and give me that
deep inner peace of forgiveness
that will enable me to pray again,
secure in the righteousness
that comes only
from abiding in Christ.

Lead us not into temptation

Temptation, testing, is bound to come to all of us. In some parts of life the tests are built in. In university, for example, there is a test at the end of the course, to see what you have learned. You know it is coming, and you have time to prepare for it. You hope that the questions will be such that they test the areas of the course that you know, and not the areas in which you are unsure. Many people would rather do away with examinations because there is some element of chance and unfairness to them. Maybe there is the unusual individual who knows it all and looks forward to exams. Here is a chance to shine and get 99%!

But the tests of life are different from school examinations. First, there is no set time. When all seems to be floating along calmly, we are struck down by disease or are afflicted by an unexpected bereavement. Our test is how we handle that, whether we let bitterness gain entry to our soul. Or maybe relationships in a group seem to be good, then unexpectedly somebody slanders us. That is a test for us! Are we going to fight fire with fire? We think we are loving, peaceful, Christian people, but are we when the test comes? And we never know when that test will come.

Second, we do not know in what area of life our test will be. Will our patience be tried, or our love or our fortitude or our honesty? Maybe we think in terms of some big test, some disaster that we shall have to suffer under, but then our test comes when somebody begins to praise us unduly and we give in to pride. It is important to face the little tests well, for they can strengthen us for any big test that might come.

Third, in the tests of life it is only the fool who boasts the ability to cope in the way a straight-A student might boast the ability to do well in an exam. I remember hearing at university of a student who was a brilliant mathematical scholar. As he was going off to his final exams, someone called out, "Good luck!" He retorted with scorn, "It's not luck I want, but justice." In life we would be foolish to adopt that kind of attitude, as though we had it all together, as though we could face anything in life as long as we got justice. There is no guarantee of justice in life. We do not all start equal. Some people seem to have all the breaks; others seem to accumulate one disaster on top of another. So in life's uncertainties we had better not boast of our ability to meet the tests of life. No wonder St Paul says, "So, if you think you are standing firm, be careful that you don't fall!" (1 Corinthians 10:12).

We are all in danger of falling. We all often fall. No wonder Jesus invites us to pray with him, "Lead us not into temptation." Jesus himself prayed, "My Father, if it is possible, may this cup be taken from me. Yet not as I will, but as you will" (Matthew 26:39).

O Lord,
The tests of life
are sometimes too much for me,
and then I come running to you.
Teach me not to wait for the big exams,
but every day
to seek your guidance and help

in facing the small tests
of my patience,
of my love,
of my faith,
of my hope.
Give me the stability
that comes from
abiding in Christ.

For thine is the kingdom, the power, and the glory, for ever and ever. Amen.

The end of prayer is not that I may get. It is not that I may achieve the status of one who prays well. The end of prayer is the glory of God. So it is most appropriate that our prayer should end, "For thine is the kingdom, the power, and the glory, for ever and ever. Amen."

Prayer is about the coming of his kingdom, about the exercise of his power, and is for his glory. The Lord's Prayer ends solidly in the acknowledgement of him, and not for us and our needs, our sinfulness and our weakness.

It is *his* kingdom. The purpose of prayer is not to build my little kingdom. Its aim is not the formation of a little world that centres in me, where my needs are met, where my success is assured, and where I am preserved from all sickness. As long as prayer is centred in me, it is not true prayer. True prayer is for the coming in its fullness of God's kingdom. True prayer is in the context of the present activity in the kingdom.

"Thy kingdom come" — on bended knee
The passing ages pray;
And faithful souls have yearned to see
On earth that kingdom's day.

That yearning is true prayer.

It is *his* power. We do not achieve in prayer. He achieves through us. Anyone who would pray must be aware of his "incomparably great power for us who believe" (Ephesians 1:19). As we learn to pray in Christ, we want more and more to say with St Paul, "Now to him who is able to do immeasurably more than all we ask or imagine, according to his power that is at work within us" (Ephesians 3:20). God has the power to do more than we ask. He does things of which we do not even think. An old prayer begins, "Almighty and everlasting God, who art always more ready to hear than we to pray, and art wont to give more than either we desire or deserve." To pray, abiding in Christ, is to be aware of God's richness towards us and of his eternal power. "Thine is the kingdom and the power."

And *his* is the glory. Paul's ascription in Ephesians finishes, "To him be glory in the church and in Christ Jesus throughout all generations, for ever and ever! Amen" (Ephesians 3:20–21). The aim of prayer is his glory. Jesus in his prayer to God on the night he was betrayed said of his earthly ministry, "I have brought you glory on earth by completing the work you gave me to do" (John 17:4). That was his purpose. Our purpose also, if we would abide in him, is by our actions, our words, and our prayers, to glorify the Father. The song of the elders in the book of Revelation, as they cast their crowns before the throne, is "You are worthy, our Lord and God, to receive glory and honor and power, for you created all things, and by your will they were created and have their being" (Revelation 4:11).

We who abide in Jesus will find that more and more our prayers will be saying, "For thine is the kingdom, the power, and the glory, for ever and ever. Amen."

O Lord,
I'm still so much at the centre
of my prayers.
Teach me to pray
so that my prayer
seeks your kingdom,
and desires your glory.

Lord, by your power,
teach me to pray,
abiding in Christ.

*The Sermon
on the Mount*

> *Now when he saw the crowds, he went up on a mountainside*
> *and sat down. His disciples came to him, and he began to teach*
> *them. (Matthew 5:1-2).*

One of the mistakes we make about prayer is to sort it off into
a separate category of life. Christian prayer is not a segment of
life, but the response of our whole lives to God. We call the focus-
ing of that relationship prayer. But the sacrifice that God calls
us to make is a living one — the presentation of our bodies, the
renewal of our minds — that we may "test and approve what
God's will is — his good, pleasing and perfect will" (Romans
12:2). The passage in the New Testament that we call the Sermon on the Mount is about prayer in its widest sense. Jesus talks
about the specifics of praying in the wider context of living. It
is a sermon about renewal, the renewal that comes from abiding
in Christ.

It's a pity that the word *renewal* has come to have a particular
flavour for some people. Parishes that have been renewed often
have the other label *charismatic*. Renewal means guitars and new
liturgies. Maybe it implies speaking in tongues and dancing round
the church. But in the New Testament, renewal is not a special-
ized form in that way. Nor does it have to do with external forms,
liturgies, and musical instruments. It does not belong to any section of the church. Renewal is what God is doing. Renewal is
for every believer. Renewal is the work of the Lord who says,
"I am making everything new" (Revelation 21:5). Renewal is the
fulfilment of the Lord's promise in Ezekiel, "I will give you a new
heart and put a new spirit in you" (Ezekiel 36:26).

There is the reality that God has created a new thing. St Paul
says, "If anyone is in Christ, he is a new creation; the old has
gone, the new has come" (2 Corinthians 5:17). We need to claim
that reality. When I am in Jesus and the Lord has come into my
heart, I am a new person before God.

There is reality here which I must claim. Paul says, "You have
put on the new self, which is being renewed in knowledge in
the image of its creator" (Colossians 3:10). I am new; God sees
me in a new light. But that newness needs to permeate my whole
being. That is seen as a twofold operation, God's work and my
work. I am being renewed by the Spirit of God, *and* I must work
at living the new life. This dual approach is seen in Ephesians

4:23-24: "Be made new in the attitude of your minds; and put on the new self, created to be like God in true righteousness and holiness." That is both opening ourselves to God's work of our being "made new" and ourselves putting on the new life.

The Sermon on the Mount is not a moral exhortation. Nor is it a new law to replace the law that Moses brought down from the mountain. Rather, the Sermon on the Mount is a description of the new person in Christ. What does it mean to live the new life? How does the new life alter our way of looking at things? How is the new life reflected in our relationships? How do we stand with God in the new life? If we can let the reality of the new life shape us, we shall find that our prayers also take on a new meaning.

O God,
too often I want less
than you would give me.
I've wanted a list of rules
on how to be a good Christian,
but you give me
a new life in Christ.
May I know that
I am your new creation,
by the new heart you have given me
and the new spirit you have put within me.
May I live that new life
which reflects your image in me,
for only in that miracle
can I be
made new in Christ.

Do not think that I have come to abolish the Law or the Pro-
phets; I have not come to abolish them but to fulfill them. I tell
you the truth, until heaven and earth disappear, not the smallest
letter, not the least stroke of a pen, will by any means disappear
from the Law until everything is accomplished. Anyone who
breaks one of the least of these commandments and teaches others
to do the same will be called least in the kingdom of heaven, but
whoever practises and teaches these commands will be called
great in the kingdom of heaven. For I tell you that unless your
righteousness surpasses that of the Pharisees and the teachers of
the law, you will certainly not enter the kingdom of heaven.
(Matthew 5:17–20)

My grandfather in one thing at least was a legalist. In England
Sunday newspapers are like our Saturday ones. They contain
more magazine articles and are in many homes an integral part
of Sunday. But my grandfather had Sunday principles which included not buying a Sunday newspaper. However, most Sun-
days on his way to church he would find occasion to call by our
house. I suspect that it was not only to see us, for he did make
time to take more than a glance at our Sunday paper!

I think some people must be born legalists. You hear them
sometimes in church discussions, and they always want to apply
the canon law. There are some dioceses where they spend hours
every Synod rewriting and expanding the canons. Everything
needs to be down in black and white. There must be a regulation
for everything. Most of us don't care for that kind of legalism.
We only want to discover the law when it has some benefit for
us. If a canon law gives us a right in a situation, we are glad to
discover it. When we find a clause in the income tax act which
we can use to give us another exemption, we are glad of the law.

Jesus speaks of law in the sermon on the mount. He spoke to
people who lived by the law, and he called them to go beyond
the law — not to live by an external code but to have a renewed
heart. Jesus says that he came to fulfill the law and the prophets.
There were some of his hearers who saw him as a threat to their
way of life. They thought that he was coming with a revolutionary
message to overthrow the existing order, and Jesus had to say
clearly to them, ''Do not think that I have come to abolish the

Law or the Prophets'' (Matthew 5:17). Jesus' message was revolutionary, but it did not overthrow what God had said in the past. Rather, Jesus called for a new interpretation of that old law, which would bring people closer to the righteousness to which the law and the prophets had pointed.

The trouble was that the law had become an end in itself. The important thing was to keep the law; that was the relationship — a relationship with the law rather than a relationship with God or my fellow man. When the law is the end, there are two dangers. The first is that I can claim to have kept it. All the regulations have been fulfilled. But our responsibilty is not to it but to God. When I come before God, I am aware of a greater mystery, a living love, before which, as Scripture puts it, ''all our righteous acts are like filthy rags'' (Isaiah 64:6).

Second, I am in serious danger when law looms larger than my neighbour, when I can see the rules and regulations but don't really see my neighbour as a person. When I can see quite clearly that ''Chapter 16, paragraph 5, subsection C'' applies, but cannot see that this man is hurting, I am in trouble. It is only when I see *him* that there is possibility of a relationship. The rules might allow us to coexist, but they will not bring the loving relationship that God intended us to have.

Jesus said, ''Unless your righteousness surpasses that of the Pharisees and the teachers of the law, you will certainly not enter the kingdom of heaven'' (Matthew 5:20). Their rightness was in relationship to law, and not to God and their neighbour. We need that law as our guide, because we are human. But it must be a guide that leads us to God and to our neighbour, rather than being a barrier that hides God and our neighbour.

There is renewal in Jesus Christ because he takes us beyond law. He shows us that God does not deal with us by law but by love. Jesus calls me to see my neighbour as someone for whom he died.

O God,
rules can be clear
and I know where I stand,

but Jesus made it clear
that life is more than rules.
The letter of the law
can kill
my relationship with you
and with my brothers and sisters.
Open my eyes to you afresh;
help me to see my neighbour
in a new light,
for only in that miracle
can I be
made new in Christ.

You have heard that it was said to the people long ago, 'Do not murder, and anyone who murders will be subject to judgement.' But I tell you that anyone who is angry with his brother will be subject to judgement. Again, anyone who says to his brother, 'Raca,' is answerable to the Sanhedrin. But anyone who says, 'You fool!' will be in danger of the fire of hell. Therefore, if you are offering your gift at the altar and there remember that your brother has something against you, leave your gift there in front of the altar. First go and be reconciled to your brother; then come and offer your gift. Settle matters quickly with your adversary who is taking you to court. Do it while you are still with him on the way, or he may hand you over to the judge, and the judge may hand you over to the officer, and you may be thrown into prison. I tell you the truth, you will not get out until you have paid the last penny. You have heard that it was said, 'Do not commit adultery.' But I tell you that anyone who looks at a woman lustfully has already committed adultery with her in his heart. If your right eye causes you to sin, gouge it out and throw it away. It is better for you to lose one part of your body than for your whole body to be thrown into hell. And if your right hand causes you to sin, cut it off and throw it away. It is better for you to lose one part of your body than for your whole body to go into hell. (Matthew 5:21–30)

Being renewed in Christ is to have a new heart. Outward actions are not the sole criteria for judgement. A person could do the right things, but unless that person's heart is changed, he or she is far from the kingdom of God.

Jesus points us to two areas of the law: "Do not murder" and "Do not commit adultery." They are very measurable acts. There can be no doubt in our minds whether we are guilty of either. Yet in Jesus there is a wholly different level. It is an area which is not so easy for the outside world to measure. It is an area of which we are all too aware and which lies open to God. It is that inner area of our minds and our secret desires. Others do not see those secret thoughts, but they are not hidden from God. We are reminded of that in the collect which begins, "Almighty God, unto whom all hearts are open, all desires known, and from whom no secrets are hid . . ."

"Do not murder" is the commandment, but Jesus says, "Anyone who is angry with his brother will be subject to judgement" (Matthew 5:22). We get upset with someone, then begin to resent him. We see all his actions as being twisted, and we insult him. Then we allow a quiet anger to grow in our hearts, and we nurse that anger. The end of that process is that we grow hard and bitter. When hardness of soul takes over, it affects our relationship not only with the man with whom we are angry, but with everyone else. It works against any open relationships. It makes us less than the persons God intended us to be.

In Jesus Christ there is the desire to reverse the process. Reconciliation is a priority. Jesus says, "If you are offering your gift at the altar and there remember that your brother has something against you, leave your gift there in front of the altar. First go and be reconciled to your brother; then come and offer your gift" (Matthew 5:23–24). Our relationship with God is dependent on our relationship with other people. That's what St John says when he writes, "If anyone says, 'I love God,' yet hates his brother, he is a liar" (1 John 4:20).

St Paul writes so often about our personal relationships. Since forgiveness is *the* characteristic of the new heart in Jesus Christ, Paul calls his readers to "bear with each other and forgive whatever grievances you may have against one another. Forgive as the Lord forgave you" (Colossians 3:13). The practical word from Paul is, "In your anger do not sin. Do not let the sun go down while you are still angry" (Ephesians 4:26)

The second area in which Jesus pushes beyond the external is our sexuality. The commandment is "Do not commit adultery." Jesus, however, says, "Anyone who looks at a woman lustfully has already committed adultery with her in his heart" (Matthew 5:28). When a man looks lustfully at a woman, he has already begun to see her not as a person to whom he must relate but as a person whom he must possess. When we look lustfully, it is *self*-satisfaction that dominates our thinking. Whenever self-satisfaction motivates any relationship, it ruins that relationship. When God gave us the gift of sexual relationships he intended it to express a one-flesh relationship, a profound mystery parallel to the relationship between Christ and the church. It is a relationship of love, forgiveness, and giving.

When I lust, I destroy in myself the possibility of the kind of relationship that God meant us to have. I pervert the person God meant me to be. That perversion of my personhood is so serious that Jesus goes on to say, "If your right eye causes you to sin, gouge it out and throw it away. It is better for you to lose one part of your body than for your whole body to be thrown into hell" (Matthew 5:29). Obviously Jesus, who has been driving at inner responses rather than external, is not to be taken literally. In his strong, picturesque language, he is speaking of the seriousness of sin, the seriousness of anything that makes us less than the persons God meant us to be. One part of me can affect the whole and drive that whole person into a hellish state. If I hate a person, it can make my whole life bitter. If I lust after a person, it can affect my other relationships, particularly my relationship with my wife.

Jesus would come into our hearts, to give us a new heart, a forgiving heart, a loving heart, a pure heart.

O God,
I know only too well that
I can keep the rules
but lose the game.

I may try to keep the commandments,
but I need to ask myself
whether I've let bitterness and anger
make their home in me.
I need to look at my relationships
to see whether
my desire is to possess,
my aim is self-satisfaction.
Lord, give me a new love,
a desire to reconcile,
an intention to give myself,
for only in that miracle
can I be
made new in Christ.

It has been said, 'Anyone who divorces his wife must give her a certificate of divorce.' But I tell you that anyone who divorces his wife, except for marital unfaithfulness, causes her to commit adultery, and anyone who marries a woman so divorced commits adultery. Again, you have heard that it was said to the people long ago, 'Do not break your oath, but keep the oaths you have made to the Lord.' But I tell you, Do not swear at all: either by heaven, for it is God's throne; or by the earth, for it is his footstool; or by Jerusalem, for it is the city of the Great King. And do not swear by your head, for you cannot make even one hair white or black. Simply let your 'Yes' be 'Yes,' and your 'No,' 'No'; anything beyond this comes from the evil one. (Matthew 5:31–37).

When I finally got over my reluctance to go to the eye doctor (fear that the aging process was catching up with me delayed that visit!) and got a pair of glasses, what a difference it made to what I saw. Beautiful things in the countryside that I thought I had been seeing, were suddenly a lot clearer than I had imagined. Our vision can be blurred by our limitations.

Similarly, our understanding of what God expects of us and intends for us is blurred sometimes by the limitations of the law. For example, the law says that divorce is an option when a marriage breaks down. Because divorce is now so common, some young people have come to consider divorce as almost a part of the whole marriage picture. "Well, if it doesn't work out," they say as they are getting married, "we will get a divorce." Fortunately, the marriage service has not been adapted to read, "till there is no longer a mutual commitment," but still stands as, "till death do us part."

Jesus speaks of divorce in the Sermon on the Mount. Although the law permits a man to give his wife a certificate of divorce, Jesus says, "Anyone who divorces his wife, except for marital unfaithfulness, causes her to commit adultery, and anyone who marries a woman so divorced commits adultery" (Matthew 5:32). Those are very strong words, and to understand them we need to look at the passage where Jesus expands on this teaching in Matthew 19 and Mark 10.

Here Jesus says that Moses gave the law about divorce only because of our "hardness of heart." It is because we are so human and so sinful, because we do insist on our own rights and our personal satisfaction, because we lie to one another and are unfaithful to one another, that marriages do sometimes break down completely. The law makes provision for that in divorce. But Jesus goes on to say, "At the beginning of creation God 'made them male and female.' 'For this reason a man will leave his father and mother and be united to his wife, and the two will become one flesh.' So they are no longer two, but one. Therefore what God has joined together, let man not separate" (Mark 10:6-9).

The intention of God was that in marriage a man and woman should enter into oneness. That would be a oneness of partnership in creation, a oneness expressed physically as a sacrament of two lives in which there is giving and sharing. It is a oneness that comes from both partners fulfilling the promise, in the words of the marriage service, "wilt thou love her, comfort her, honour and keep her, in sickness and in health; and, forsaking all other, keep thee only unto her, so long as you both shall live?" Anything that destroys that marriage relationship can be classified as adultery, as the breaking of God's intention for us, as sin.

Always Jesus is calling to the fundamental level. The law, with its provisions for our hardness of heart, is not the fundamental level. We are always called back to what it is that God wants of us. Anything less is sin. At the heart of the marriage covenant there must be trust. It is not just a matter of keeping a vow made at the ceremony. That can become hollow, with a minimum observance. Any real marriage has to grow to deeper levels where each partner can trust the other. There has to be an honesty where words mean what they say. A simple *yes* has to be *yes*, and *no* has to be *no*. When words don't correspond with the intention of what a husband or wife wants to say, a marriage begins to disintegrate and may come to divorce.

Jesus calls us to a deeper honesty in relationships and to a new level of commitment to one another.

O God,
I so easily let
the level of my weakness
be my standard.
May I become more deeply aware that
I am made in your image
and that you are always calling me
to be a loving person,
discovering the unity that is in Jesus,
for only in that miracle
can I be
made new in Christ.

You have heard that it was said, 'Eye for eye, and tooth for tooth.' But I tell you, Do not resist an evil person. If someone strikes you on the right cheek, turn to him the other also. And if someone wants to sue you and take your tunic, let him have your cloak as well. If someone forces you to go one mile, go with him two miles. Give to the one who asks you, and do not turn away from the one who wants to borrow from you. You have heard that it was said, 'Love your neighbour and hate your enemy.' But I tell you: Love your enemies and pray for those who persecute you, that you may be sons of your Father in heaven. He causes his sun to rise on the evil and the good, and sends rain on the righteous and the unrighteous. If you love those who love you, what reward will you get? Are not even the tax collectors doing that? And if you greet only your brothers, what are you doing more than others? Do not even pagans do that? Be perfect, therefore, as your heavenly Father is perfect. (Matthew 5:38–48)

Justice is equality for all. We are all treated on the same basis. But when equality means "tit for tat," it falls short of God's intention for us in our living together. An old standard of equality was, "Eye for eye, and tooth for tooth." Justice meant, "Love your neighbour and hate your enemy." That standard only continues enmity and division among peoples. The revenged eye only encourages further retribution. Hatred breeds hatred. Revenge and hatred have been key marks of our disfigurement of the image of God in us down through the centuries. They have been reflected in personal and national histories. So many murders are the result of someone getting his own back. So many wars are a continuation of past wars; after a few years the defeated side gets new resources together.

The Lord Jesus Christ calls us to a new way of thinking. In a very radical way he says, "Do not resist an evil person. If someone strikes you on the right cheek, turn to him the other also. And if someone wants to sue you and take your tunic, let him have your cloak as well. If someone forces you to go one mile, go with him two miles. Give to the one who asks you, and do not turn away from the one who wants to borrow from you" (Matthew 5:39–42). It is a matter, Jesus says, of loving your enemies and praying for those who persecute you.

For most of us it seems impossible counsel. We cannot conceive going beyond holding our peace when we are offended. To turn the other cheek when one is struck, to give the cloak when your coat is taken, to go the second mile when one mile is forced from you, seem to be the way of suicide. The example of the Father in making the sun rise on the evil and the good, and the rain fall on the just and the unjust, does not stir most of us to a new way of acting. We need more than example. Jesus ends this section by saying, "Be perfect, therefore, as your heavenly Father is perfect" (Matthew 5:48). We are called to be like the Father, for we are made in his image. Jesus never lets us be content with ourselves as we are, or with some reasonable standard. He always calls us to be what we were meant to be.

Jesus reflected the Father in his own life in his treatment of his enemies. That was not a pattern of being a doormat. When some Pharisees came and said to him, "Leave this place and go somewhere else. Herod wants to kill you," Jesus said, "Go tell that fox, 'I will drive out demons and heal people today and tomorrow, and on the third day I will reach my goal' " (Luke 13:31–32). It was not the time to lay down his life. Or earlier in his ministry, when the people at Nazareth were furious at his words, "They got up, drove him out of the town, and took him to the brow of the hill on which the town was built, in order to throw him down the cliff" (Luke 4:29), Jesus did not just hand himself over to his enemies. Instead, "He walked right through the crowd and went on his way" (Luke 4:30). Yet when the time came for his life to be sacrificed, he died praying, "Father forgive them, for they do not know what they are doing" (Luke 23:34).

When you look at Jesus' life, you can see that he is not giving us rules and regulations for the treatment of our enemies, but is calling us to a new way of life which is marked by forgiveness, by taking the first and the subsequent steps towards reconciliation, and by prayer. St Paul puts it, "Do not be overcome by evil, but overcome evil with good" (Romans 12:21). Yet we are not left just with the examples of the Father's generosity and Jesus' way of forgiveness. The mystery of being renewed in Christ is that he can enter our hearts, and his love and forgiveness begin to grow in us.

O God,
when I am wronged
I want not only
to stand up for my rights
but somehow to push the other person down.
My nature wants to continue the war
till I am vindicated.
This pattern can only destroy your world.
Teach me a new way,
and by your Spirit give me a new heart of love,
so that I may begin to forgive,
to take the first step in apologizing,
and to uphold in prayer before you
those who misunderstand and wrong me;
for only in that miracle
can I be
made new in Christ.

Be careful not do your 'acts of righteousness' before men, to be seen by them. If you do, you will have no reward from your Father in heaven. So when you give to the needy, do not announce it with trumpets, as the hypocrites do in the synagogues and on the streets, to be honoured by men. I tell you the truth, they have received their reward in full. But when you give to the needy, do not let your left hand know what your right hand is doing, so that your giving may be in secret. Then your Father, who sees what is done in secret, will reward you. But when you pray, do not be like the hypocrites, for they love to pray standing in the synagogues and on the street corners to be seen by men. I tell you the truth, they have received their reward in full. When you pray, go into your room, close the door and pray to your Father, who is unseen. Then your Father, who sees what is done in secret, will reward you. And when you

*pray, do not keep on babbling like pagans, for they think they
will be heard because of their many words. Do not be like them,
for your Father knows what you need before you ask him.''
(Matthew 6:1–8)*

*When you fast, do not look somber as the hypocrites do, for they
disfigure their faces to show men they are fasting. I tell you the
truth, they have received their reward in full. But when you
fast, put oil on your head and wash your face, so that it will not
be obvious to men that you are fasting, but only to your Father,
who is unseen; and your Father, who sees what is done in
secret, will reward you. (Matthew 6:16–18)*

Renewal in Christ means getting a new focus in our praying. Jesus
speaks about people who practise their piety before men in order
to be seen by them. They give with ostentation, so that men will
be impressed. They "love to pray standing in the synagogues and
on the street corners to be seen by men" (Matthew 6:5). We are
horrified by such a picture. We would not dream of blowing a
trumpet before we put our offering in the plate. We would never
think of stopping to pray aloud in the middle of a downtown
street.

Perhaps our reasons for not acting in this way are not just horror
at the practices of those hypocrites in Jesus' day. Maybe we would
not think of publicizing our offering because there really is not
very much to blow a trumpet about. Our generosity in church
too often looks very thin beside what we spend on our entertain-
ment. Maybe we would not pray in public because we are rather
self-conscious about our praying. We would not want anyone to
think we were strangely religious. Our thin times of prayer do
not give us much confidence to pray aloud before others. So we
had better think twice before pointing the finger of judgement
at those hypocrites of Jesus' day.

The whole issue is one of motivation. The hypocrites prayed
and gave for their own ends. They wanted to be seen by men
and to be praised. How much of our lives are caught up with
making an impression on other people? We think that life is about
making an impression on others. But being renewed in Christ
brings the conviction that we have worth because God loves us

and not because of the impression we make. Much advertizing is geared to the thought of our making an impression. We wear the latest fashion to impress. Our car and our home can leave the impression of affluence and success. We succumb to these images. We want to be accepted.

I remember as a parish priest going to visit a home. It was an affluent home, all newly furnished; it had that look of comfortable luxury. Here was a man moving up the corporate scale. A few months later, when the marriage broke up, I came to learn that absolutely nothing was paid for and there was really nothing to pay the bills. The picture of a contented family was also part of the image, but there was no reality behind the picture.

That was an extreme case, but in so many ways the reality is very close to us. We want to make an impression so that we will be accepted. We get caught up with the image, and we fiddle about with the externals, while the inside is empty. Or we judge other people by the externals — the clothes, the mannerisms, their associations. We never even give the real person underneath a chance to emerge.

But let us not fool ourselves. God is not deceived. We cannot make an impression on him by our piety or religion. Men may be impressed, but not God. God accepts us in his love, and not because we look good. St Paul says, "But because of his great love for us, God, who is rich in mercy, made us alive with Christ even when we were dead in transgressions" (Ephesians 2:4–5). That alters the whole nature of our praying and our living. Making a good impression is not our focus. Rather, praying and living are a response to the impress that God has put on us in Jesus Christ, for he has made us alive and gives us a new nature.

O God,
I've sometimes thought
I could get away with
a good impression.
The externals have all been there,
but there's been an emptiness inside.
May I know that
it is by the greatness of your love

I am ultimately accepted;
then I can be myself
in touch with reality,
reaching out in love,
for only in that miracle
can I be
made new in Christ.

---

*Do not store up for yourselves treasures on earth, where moth
and rust destroy, and where thieves break in and steal. But store
up for yourselves treasures in heaven, where moth and rust do
not destroy, and where thieves do not break in and steal. For
where your treasure is, there your heart will be also. The eye is
the lamp of the body. If your eyes are good, your whole body
will be full of light. But if your eyes are bad, your whole body
will be full of darkness. If then the light within you is darkness,
how great is that darkness! No one can serve two masters. Either
he will hate the one and love the other, or he will be devoted to
the one and despise the other. You cannot serve both God and
Money. Therefore I tell you, do not worry about your life, what
you will eat or drink; or about your body, what you will wear.
Is not life more important than food, and the body more important than clothes? Look at the birds of the air; they do not sow
or reap or store away in barns, and yet your heavenly Father
feeds them. Are you not much more valuable then they? Who of
you by worrying can add a single hour to his life? And why do
you worry about clothes? See how the lilies of the field grow.
They do not labour or spin. Yet I tell you that not even Solomon
in all his splendour was dressed like one of these. If that is how
God clothes the grass of the field, which is here today and
tomorrow is thrown into the fire, will he not much more clothe
you, O you of little faith? So do not worry, saying, 'What shall
we eat?' or 'What shall we drink?' or 'What shall we wear?' For
the pagans run after all these things, and your heavenly Father*

knows that you need them. But seek first his kingdom and his
righteousness, and all these things will be given to you as well.
Therefore do not worry about tomorrow, for tomorrow will worry
about itself. Each day has enough trouble of its own. (Matthew
6:19-34)

When we say, "He's got his eye on a new car," we mean that
he has been thinking a lot about a new car recently, that he has
probably seen something that takes his fancy, and that in all pro-
bability he will end up buying it. I wondered for a while what
the two verses about the eye being the lamp of the body were
doing sandwiched between a paragraph about laying up treasure
in heaven and a paragraph on being anxious about things. I
thought at first that Matthew must have got these verses out of
context. Then the penny dropped, and I saw that the question
for us is, What do we have our eye on?

Jesus said, "The eye is the lamp of the body. If your eyes are
good, your whole body will be full of light. But if your eyes are
bad, your whole body will be full of darkness. If then the light
within you is darkness, how great is that darkness!" (Matthew
6:22-23). If our eye is fixed on things, there will be a darkness
in our whole personality. If our eye is fixed on God, if we will
let Jesus be the light of our world, there will be a light within
ourselves.

If our eye is on things, we shall want to store up treasures on
earth. We will want to acquire more and more, but the more we
have, the more we have to worry about. The more gadgets we
have, the more can go wrong. The more valuable things we have,
the more we have to be concerned that they are not stolen, and
the more we will have to look after them to keep them from moth
and rust and from any deterioration. We all know how much time
we can spend on possessions. Things can take over in our lives.
Concern for things can fill our hearts, so that people begin to take
a second place. Parents work to get a new TV, a second car, a
country place, and have no time for their children. They just
assume that they will grow. And when concern for things fills
our lives, God also is squeezed out. There is not time to pray.
There is not time to worship in church. Jesus says, "Where your
treasure is, there your heart will be also" (Matthew 6:21).

When we begin to let money, or our things, dominate our lives, we cannot also be under the lordship of God. Jesus says, "No one can serve two masters . . . You cannot serve both God and Money" (Matthew 6:24). I am sure we would all protest that we do not serve money. Yet we need to reassess our lives and the time we spend on things. How large a priority in our lives is our desire for things or our care for things we do possess? Is our eye on things or on God?

When our eye is on things, we begin to think that our security lies in things: in our money, our pension plan, our savings, our house. So we become anxious. When we become anxious, things take up more of our time. Of course, there is no ultimate security in things. Savings can become worthless, a house can burn, an earthquake can topple our work, sickness can strike without any warning. We have no security except in God. St Paul writes, "Who shall separate us from the love of Christ? Shall trouble or hardship or persecution or famine or nakedness or danger or sword?" (Romans 8:35). There is no guarantee of escape from calamity. St Paul had known his fill of disasters, yet he goes on to say, "For I am convinced that neither death nor life, neither angels nor demons, neither the present nor the future, nor any powers, neither height nor depth, nor anything else in all creation, will be able to separate us from the love of God that is in Christ Jesus our Lord" (Romans 8:38–39). That is our security.

Our lives will be renewed as we turn our eyes to look up to God, who is our heavenly Father, who knows our needs, who feeds the birds, and who clothes the lilies of the field.

O God,
I've spent too much time
looking at things,
desiring things,
caring for things.
They have begun to dominate my life.
Yet they cannot be my master
if I would call you Master.

Become to me the Light
so that my whole life
may be renewed,
for only in that miracle
can I be
made new in Christ.

---

*Do not judge, or you too will be judged. For in the same way
you judge others, you will be judged, and with the measure you
use, it will be measured to you. Why do you look at the speck of
sawdust in your brother's eye and pay no attention to the plank
in your own eye? How can you say to your brother, 'Let me take
the speck out of your eye,' when all the time there is a plank in
your own eye? You hypocrite, first take the plank out of your
own eye, and then you will see clearly to remove the speck from
your brother's eye. Do not give dogs what is sacred; do not
throw your pearls to pigs. If you do, they may trample them
under their feet, and then turn and tear you to pieces (Matthew
7:1–6).*

The see-saw theory of human nature is very much in vogue. By
pushing the other person down, I push myself up. If I can see
his faults, I don't look half bad. I say to someone about my rival,
"Yes, he's fine *but* . . ." and there follows a list of his faults. And
there's the implication that I don't have these faults. We become
judgemental people to bolster our own image, which in reality
means that we become hard-hearted and blind. We're so blind
we cannot see the log in our own eye. What a wonderful picture
that is which Jesus gives! It is one of those laughable pictures that
people remember. A man with a great log in his eye pointing to
the speck in his brother's eye!

Even as we laugh at this word-picture, we know it to be true.
The person who becomes very conscious of others' faults all too

often becomes blind to his own. We see that happening to others, and we are surprised that our friends can be unaware of their own faults. Of course, others often see that same characteristic in us.

Jesus wasn't against the exercise of judgement. He goes on immediately, to say, "Do not give dogs what is sacred; do not throw your pearls to pigs" (Matthew 7:6). We need to exercise judgement, to discern good from evil, the holy from the profane, the truth from the lie. Every day in my work I make judgements about what I will do, about whom I will trust. What Jesus is talking about is the judgemental attitude. That attitude is always looking for the bad, always finding something to criticize. The person with a judgemental attitude forgets that he is under judgement. We live before God who knows our inmost thoughts. Our lives lie open before him, for he does not judge by what the eye sees, but he knows the whole situation. He knows the opportunities we have had and the drawbacks we have had to face.

God does not judge me in comparison with my brother. It is not how I stand compared with anyone else. My sins are not overlooked because they are not as bad as someone else's. So St Paul can write, "There is no difference, for all have sinned and fall short of the glory of God" (Romans 3:22–23). It is when we realize that we are under judgement that a change begins to take place in our hearts, a change that can make us realize how much God has forgiven us. It is a change that begins to make us more merciful and that encourages us to look for the good.

O God,
it's so easy to try to bolster myself
by pushing someone down.
There are some people
in whom I can see only
things to criticize.
Help me to remember
that I am under your judgement
and that I have been forgiven,
so that I may have new eyes

to see your goodness working in others,
for only in that miracle
can I be
made new in Christ.

---

*Ask and it will be given to you; seek and you will find; knock
and the door will be opened to you. For everyone who asks
receives; he who seeks finds; and to him who knocks, the door
will be opened. Which of you, if his son asks for bread, will give
him a stone? Or if he asks for a fish, will give him a snake? If
you, then, though you are evil, know how to give good gifts to
your children, how much more will your Father in heaven give
good gifts to those who ask him! In everything, do to others
what you would have them do to you, for this sums up the Law
and the Prophets. (Matthew 7:7–12).*

Sometimes it is difficult to ask. We want to be self-sufficient.
The reality is that self-sufficiency is an illusion. We can never be
self-sufficient. We are dependent on one another, and we are
dependent on our heavenly Father.

Part of growing up is learning independence. A baby begins
to want to do it himself — to feed himself, to walk by himself,
to dress himself. There is a natural and necessary frustration at
being helped. A young person begins to stand on his own two
feet, making decisions, taking actions on his own. The break from
the nest is important. Yet once we are grown up and independent we have to learn in a deeper way the reality of our need
for one another's help, the reality of our need for God. If we do
not, we miss out on what life is about. Our self-sufficiency tends
to make us hard and aloof. We miss that ministry to our needs
that could bring a healing to our lives.

This paragraph of the sermon speaks of our dependence on
God. Our Father in heaven, Jesus teaches us, is more than will-

ing to give good things to those who ask him. He is more concerned than any earthly father for his children.

Why don't we ask? Firstly, there is that sense of self-sufficiency. We can work it out on our own. We do not want to be obligated to anybody. But how foolish that is! We are obligated to God from the very beginning of our lives. The whole miracle of birth and growth is the gift of God. The beauty of the world around us is the gift of God. The food we eat (although there was human effort in the planting and reaping and processing) is dependent on that miracle of growth from God. The air we breathe, the very life we live, is the gift of God. How can we pretend to be independent?

Secondly, we do not ask the Lord because we do not trust his goodness towards us. Sometimes people say that, even if there is a life force, it cannot be concerned with us and our needs. But the Christian message, if it says anything, says that God is concerned about me as an individual and that his attitude towards me is one of love. How could God say that more strongly than by giving his Son to die? Jesus taught us not about God as a principle but about God as our Father. Once Jesus has entered our heart and given us a new heart, we know we can come to our Father and ask for what we need. Sometimes our Father will say no, for our own good. But we know we can ask.

This confidence in coming to God is expressed in the letter to the Hebrews: "Therefore, brothers, since we have confidence to enter the Most Holy Place by the blood of Jesus, by a new and living way opened for us through the curtain, that is his body, and since we have a great priest over the house of God, let us draw near to God with a sincere heart in full assurance of faith, having our hearts sprinkled to cleanse us from a guilty conscience and having our bodies washed with pure water" (Hebrews 10:19-22). We can come to our Father in Jesus.

But coming to our Father implies also coming to our brothers and sisters in Christ. There is a new relationship of giving and receiving. Jesus says, "In everything, do to others what you would have them do to you" (Matthew 7:12). This follows on the Father's goodness to us. A new heart open to God's goodness to us is also a new heart open to others to give and to receive in love.

O God,
in my pride I want to be self-sufficient.
It's so easy to forget how dependent I am
on you and on others.
Give me a new vision of your loving goodness
that I may trustfully turn to you in prayer,
and be willing to receive
your love through others,
for only in that miracle
can I be
made new in Christ.

Enter through the narrow gate. For wide is the gate and broad is the road that leads to destruction, and many enter through it. But small is the gate and narrow the road that leads to life, and only a few find it. Watch out for false prophets. They come to you in sheep's clothing, but inwardly they are ferocious wolves. By their fruit you will recognize them. Do people pick grapes from thornbushes, or figs from thistles? Likewise every good tree bears good fruit, but a bad tree bears bad fruit. A good tree cannot bear bad fruit, and a bad tree cannot bear good fruit. Every tree that does not bear good fruit is cut down and thrown into the fire. Thus, by their fruit you will recognize them. Not everyone who says to me, 'Lord, Lord,' will enter the kingdom of heaven, but only he who does the will of my Father who is in heaven. Many will say to me on that day, 'Lord, Lord, did we not prophesy in your name, and in your name drive out demons and perform many miracles?' Then I will tell them plainly, 'I never knew you. Away from me, you evildoers!' Therefore everyone who hears these words of mine and puts them into practice is like a wise man who built his house on the rock. The rain came down, the streams rose, and the winds blew and beat against that house; yet it did not fall, because it had its founda-

tion on the rock. But everyone who hears these words of mine
and does not put them into practice is like a foolish man who
built his house on sand. The rain came down, the streams rose,
and the winds blew and beat against that house, and it fell with
a great crash. (Matthew 7:13–27)

Words! Words can sound so convincing, so intellectual, so
religious. But our faith is in the Word that became flesh. Those
who acknowledge that Word are called to incarnate his words
— that is, to put flesh on them, to show them, as he did, in the
daily actions of life. The real test is the life, and not the words:
"Not everyone who says to me, 'Lord, Lord,'" says Jesus, "will
enter the kingdom of heaven, but only he who does the will of
my Father who is in heaven." (Matthew 7:21).

These words of Jesus are a reminder that being obedient to
Christ is not easy. It is relatively easy to hear the words, to do
and say the externals; but has there been a real change? The Lord
talks of two tests. The first is the fruit. What is the result of faith
in our lives? St Paul says that the fruit of the Spirit of God is "love,
joy, peace, patience, kindness, goodness, faithfulness, gentleness,
and self-control" (Galatians 5:22). There is something real happening if we begin more and more to display those characteristics.
Notice that these are not just a list of nine things Christians must
do. Rather, they are the result, the fruit, of truly opening our
hearts to be remade and renewed by the Lord Jesus through his
Holy Spirit.

The second test is the crisis. How real is our faith when
everything seems to fall apart? Is our faith built on God who is
the rock, or on words which are shifting and unstable as sand?
Jesus tells his parable of the two houses, one built on rock, the
other on sand. The rain fell, the winds blew, and the floods came.
The house built on sand was swept away, but the house whose
foundation was in rock held.

The storm comes to all of us in one way or another. For some
Christians it has been a dreadful persecution and martyrdom. For
others it has been the tragedy of losing a beloved child or the
agony of seeing a child get into drugs and a destructive lifestyle.
For others it is being part of a church that has split over dif-

ferences. For others it is seeing a minister whom you have trusted going against everything he taught.

One way or another the storms come. Whether our faith stands depends on whether it is at the word level, the idea level, or whether a deeper change has taken place in our hearts. Our faith will only stand if day by day we have invited the Lord to dwell in us and renew us, so that we might do what he teaches.

O God,
I know the words,
I say the words,
I call you "Lord."
May you so become Lord to me
that my words become incarnate.
Let my faith be rooted and grounded
in your love,
so that I bring forth
the fruit of the Spirit today
and stand firm in the day of testing,
for only in that miracle
can I be
made new in Christ.

Blessed are the poor in spirit, for theirs is the kingdom of heaven.
Blessed are those who mourn, for they will be comforted.
Blessed are the meek, for they will inherit the earth.
Blessed are those who hunger and thirst for righteousness, for they will be filled.
Blessed are the merciful, for they will be shown mercy.
Blessed are the pure in heart, for they will see God.
Blessed are the peacemakers, for they will be called sons of God.

Blessed are those who are persecuted because of righteouness, for theirs is the kingdom of heaven.
Blessed are you when people insult you, persecute you, and falsely say all kinds of evil against you because of me. Rejoice and be glad, because great is your reward in heaven, for in the same way they persecuted the prophets who were before you.
You are the salt of the earth. But if the salt loses its saltiness, how can it be made salty again? It is no longer good for anything, except to be thrown out and trampled by men. You are the light of the world. A city on a hill cannot be hidden. Neither do people light a lamp and put it under a bowl. Instead they put it on its stand, and it gives light to everyone in the house. In the same way, let your light shine before men, that they may see your good deeds and praise your Father in heaven. (Matthew 5:3–16)

You will have wondered about the omission of the Beatitudes from the consideration of the sermon so far. They come at the beginning of the sermon as Jesus delivered it, but we do well to reread them at the end of the sermon, because they are a wonderful summary of what it means to be a new person in Christ. To be renewed by abiding in Christ is the happiness described in the Beatitudes. We read these few verses, and it is clear that they are not a new set of commandments. There's only one new commandment, which Jesus says is "Love one another. As I have loved you, so you must love one another" (John 13:34).

The Beatitudes are not a set of rules that I can cross off as I do them. Rather, they describe a new state of life, an experience that grows out of keeping the commandment of love, a way of life that reflects the reality, "If anyone is in Christ, he is a new creation; the old has gone, the new has come! All this is from God, who reconciled us to himself through Christ" (2 Corinthians 5:17–18). Blessedness — happiness — comes from what God has done. It is an awareness that God loves me, that God has put me right with himself, that God has reconciled me to himself. I do not therefore need to prove myself. I do not need to assert myself and put someone else down. There is room for all of us in God's love.

When we know in our hearts that God has taken the initiative, how can it be described? It means entering the kingdom of heaven, knowing that he is King and that all things are ultimately in his hands.

It means knowing his comfort. When St Paul went through such a rough time that he "despaired even of life" (2 Corinthians 1:9), he realized it was so that "we might not rely on ourselves but on God, who raises the dead" (2 Corinthians 1:10).

It means inheriting the earth. The earth is the Lord's and all the fullness thereof. We are aware that the world is God's good creation. We are aware that in Jesus we are fellow-heirs.

It means being satisfied. For what we basically long for is God. St Augustine wrote, "Our hearts are restless until they find their rest in thee." We were made for God, and only in him will the deep dissatisfaction in our souls find healing.

It means obtaining mercy — living in that healing sense that we are forgiven by God. We know in our very inner being that "the Lord is compassionate and gracious . . . he does not treat us as our sins deserve or repay us according to our iniquities" (Psalm 103:8, 10).

It means seeing God. St Paul puts it, "For God, who said, 'Let light shine out of darkness,' made his light shine in our hearts to give us the light of the knowledge of the glory of God in the face of Christ" (2 Corinthians 4:6). And seeing God in Jesus is a renewing process: "We who . . . all reflect the Lord's glory, are being transformed into his likeness with ever-increasing glory" (2 Corinthians 3:18).

It means being called sons and daughters of God. It is to enter into that relationship with God where, with Jesus, we can call God "Abba, Father."

In this glorious state of being God's children, of seeing him as the Lord of love, of knowing his mercy, of being satisfied, of inheriting the earth, of knowing his comfort, of entering his kingdom, there arises a new way of life. It grows out of relationship with God, rather than being a new set of rules. It is that new spirit that God has put within us, the new heart God has given us, demonstrating their reality in our lives.

So there is poverty of spirit, for we know the reality of our dependence on God.

There is mourning, for we know how we have grieved the Spirit of God within us.

There is meekness, for in Jesus, who in his meekness took the form of a servant, we realize that service comes not from weakness but from strength.

There is hunger and thirst for righteousness, for we know that God has attributed to us the righteousness of Jesus, and we want to live that righteousness.

There is purity of heart, for the eyes of our hearts (to use a biblical phrase) have been opened, and in seeing God we have a clear intention to fulfil his will.

There is the capacity to be a peacemaker, for we have known the love and forgiveness of God, of a God who accepts us as his children. That's the beginning of our being able to accept others.

There is persecution for righteousness' sake and rejection, for in the world there is still a rebellion against God, and people will not accept his law.

But all of these characteristics of the new life are blessed; in them we are happy. The Beatitudes are not rules we reluctantly struggle to obey, but rather they arise out of our rejoicing in God, who loves us so much and has become to us a present reality. We rejoice "because God has poured out his love into our hearts by the Holy Spirit, whom he has given us" (Romans 5:5). No wonder we are called to be salt of the earth and light of the world! That's not because of our own goodness but because of the Lord, the Spirit, who dwells within us.

O God,
happiness is finding you,
knowing your love,
becoming your child in Jesus, and
experiencing your Holy Spirit
in my heart.
May the vision of you
give a new light in my life.
As your child in Jesus
may I know
a new relationship
with my brothers and sisters.

May that Spirit overflow
into all my life.
Then I shall be blessed,
for only in that miracle
can I be
a new person in Christ.

The Ten
Commandments

When I was first ordained, I worked as a chaplain at McGill University. One of the the things we used to do sometimes in student discussion groups was to pick up a word or idea, and then people around the room would quickly in turn say their first association with that word. If you took the word *Christianity*, it was almost inevitable that two or three people would say, "The ten commandments." That wouldn't happen today. It happened in those days because the eucharist began with the collect for purity and then the reading of the ten commandments. I am not sure whether some of those students switched off at that point, but that was what they remembered.

It always troubled me deeply when I got that response from some who had been to church through the years, for of course our faith is not in the commandments. And yet, I think that the church has lost something in its neglect of the commandments. I suspect that many young people in the church know very little about them. The commandments were not abrogated by our Lord's coming but were put into a different context. The commandments came as the word of the Lord, and they still stand so that the people of God might be guided by this word.

The problem, as St Paul pointed out in Romans, was not with the commandments, but with us as people. Paul said, "We know that the law is spiritual; but I am unspiritual, sold as a slave to sin" (Romans 7:14). It is our human nature that is the problem. We receive the commandments, but we tend to twist them. The people of God down through the years have often been tempted to use the commandments to build their relationship with God. It was by their virtue in keeping the commandments, in living a good life, that they saw that they might build a ladder to God, that they might build a relationship with God. But, as St Paul wrote, "All have sinned and fall short of the glory of God" (Romans 3:23). The commandments do not take us to God, for we always fall short of that which God would have us be. We take the commandments and we make them measured rules. We have a self-justifying streak in us, and so we say, "Well, it was a white lie!" We explain, "I borrowed it," when we know it would be truer to admit that "I stole it."

Jesus wouldn't let people live by measured rules. He kept pushing at the commandments and saying, "You have heard that it was said to the people long ago, 'Do not murder, and anyone who murders will be subject to judgement'" (Matthew 5:21). That lets most of us off, for we have never murdered anyone. But Jesus continues, "But I tell you that anyone who is angry with his brother will be liable to judgement" (Matthew 5:22). Jesus says, "You have heard that it was said, 'Do not commit adultery.' But I tell you that anyone who looks at a woman lustfully has already committed adultery with her in his heart" (Matthew 5:27–28). He talked about divorce. He said that in the law there were provisions made for divorce: "It has been said, 'Anyone who divorces his wife must give her a certificate of divorce" (Matthew 5:31). But Jesus said that was because of the hardness of our hearts, and so he continues, "But I tell you that anyone who divorces his wife, except for marital unfaithfulness, causes her to commit adultery, and anyone who marries a women so divorced commits adultery" (Matthew 5:32). These are hard words, but Jesus always points us beyond the legal code to what God really wants of us in our lives.

When we see what is asked of us, we could despair, but there is another side to the whole matter. What the law could not do, God has done. Paul writes in Romans, "But now a righteousness from God, apart from law, has been made known" (Romans 3:21). This righteousness is the righteousness that comes in Jesus Christ. "This righteousness from God comes through faith in Jesus Christ to all who believe" (Romans 3:22). Thus, in our sinfulness, God has manifested his righteousness, his righteousness of love and forgiveness. Paul says, "He did this to demonstrate his justice, because in his forbearance he had left the sins committed beforehand unpunished" (Romans 3:25). So Christian moralism is not a response to the law which God gave, but a response to the righteousness which God has shown in Jesus Christ.

St Paul takes up the first eleven chapters of Romans writing about that righteousness, about the fact that we have fallen short of the glory of God, and also about the reality that God has forgiven us and has poured his love into our hearts through the Holy Spirit. God has acted on our behalf, and God has loved us. Having said all that, at the beginning of Romans 12, Paul continues, "Therefore, I urge you, brothers, in view of God's mercy, to offer your bodies as living sacrifices, holy and pleasing to God — which is your spiritual worship. Do not conform any longer to the pattern of this world, but be transformed by the renewing of your mind. Then you will be able to test and approve what God's will is — his good, pleasing and perfect will'' (Romans 12:1-2). Through the next three chapters he writes about what that means for our lives as Christians. The way we treat one another, forgive one another, and love one another arises as a consequence of God's love. Because of what God has done, because God has shown his love for us, we in response should seek to love God and seek to love our neighbours.

Paul, in Romans, tells us that the commandments are summed up in love. He says, ''Let no debt remain outstanding, except the continuing debt to love one another, for he who loves his fellow man has fulfilled the law. The commandments, 'Do not commit adultery,' 'Do not murder,' 'Do not steal,' 'Do not covet,' and whatever other commandment there may be, are summed up in this one rule: 'Love your neighbour as yourself.' Love does no harm to its neighbour. Therefore love is the fulfillment of the law''(Romans 13:8-10).

There is something to be said for using the summary in our modern liturgies. Jesus said that the commandments could be summed up in those two great commandments that we should love the Lord our God with all our heart and mind and soul and strength, and that we should love our neighbour as ourselves. Love grows in response. It is as I experience my wife's love for me that I love her, and it is as she experiences my love for her that she loves me. In the same way, as our hearts are open to God's love, as we hear the story of his love, as we come to know that reality in our hearts, we respond in love. This is not something that is forced; we do not need to earn anything or to win our way with God, but simply to make the response of love brought forth by God's own love.

The following meditations use the commandments as guidelines in our response to God. We are responding to God's love, which can only be real in us as we abide in Christ. These are longer meditations than in the previous sections of the book, but that has been necessary to develop the topics. Their aim is still the same: to stimulate thought in our response to God and so to lead into prayer.

O God,
when measured by your law
I know that I fall short
of the glory
you meant me to have.
Your new law never lets me
be content
with a superficial legalism.
I would despair
except for the gospel of your love.
The wonder is that
you love me
as I am.
May I so know your love
that it kindles a love in me
that begins to transform
my life,
my desires,
and all my actions
in Jesus.

---

1 I am the Lord your God, who brought you out of the land of Egypt, out of the house of bondage. You shall have no other Gods before me.

At first glance the commandments appear to start on an easy level. Not having other gods or taking the Lord's name in vain may seem to make fewer demands than telling the truth or being faithful in marriage. Maybe those early Israelites needed warning about other gods, but surely that's not a problem for us. When we get as far as number 10 and wanting what somebody else has, we've reached a universal problem! It could sound like a high jump competition, with each hurdle getting a little higher! The reality is, however, that the first commandment is the one that sums up the universal problem. We all fall at the first hurdle. There is "another god" in everyone's life. That other god is "me."

The story of Adam and Eve is at the beginning of the Bible because it describes the universal human condition. Adam and Eve did not mind having God around, but they did not want him to be God. They did not want him to be the ultimate authority. The serpent asked Eve, "Did God really say 'You must not eat from any tree in the garden?' " The fact that there was one tree from which they could not eat irked Eve. The serpent pointed out the irony of them being ruled by God in this way: "God knows that when you eat of it your eyes will be opened, and you will be like God, knowing good and evil." Adam and Eve could be their own gods. They could determine for themselves what was right and wrong.

That is really a story about the human race. There come times in all our lives when we want to go our own way. We have heard the word of the Lord, but we are determined to make up our own minds about what is right and wrong. We will be our own God.

In the Bible, the story that is set in contrast to Adam and Eve is that of Jesus Christ. Paul sums up Jesus' life in the letter to the Philippians. He wrote that Jesus, "being in very nature God, did not consider equality with God something to be grasped, but made himself nothing, taking the very nature of a servant, being made in human likeness. And being found in appearance as a man, he humbled himself and became obedient to death" (Philippians 2:6-8). Unlike Eve, Jesus did not count equality with God something to be grasped.

Right at the beginning of his ministry this is made clear. Jesus went into the wilderness where the devil tempted him in three ways, trying to make him put himself first. Jesus points on each occasion to the word of God. Tempted to turn stones into bread, he says, "Man does not live on bread alone, but on every word that comes from the mouth of God" (Matthew 4:4). To the temptation to prove God's providence by throwing himself from the temple pinnacle, Jesus replies, "It is also written; Do not put the Lord your God to the test" (Matthew 5:7). Finally, the devil offers Jesus the kingdoms of the world in exchange for his homage, and

Jesus replies, "It is written: Worship the Lord your God, and serve him only" (Matthew 5:10).

Jesus very consciously sought to be in the Father's will. He said to his disciples, "My food is to do the will of him who sent me and to finish his work" (John 4:34). Or again, when he suspected that people would try to make him king after he had fed the multitude, he slipped away and taught his disciples, "I have come down from heaven not to do my will, but to do the will of him who sent me" (John 6:38). When doing that will led to Gethsemane, his prayer was, "Father, if you are willing, take this cup from me; yet not my will, but yours be done" (Luke 22:42).

To be a follower of Jesus means following that pattern he showed us. Paul's advice to us is, "Your attitude should be the same as that of Christ Jesus" (Philippians 2:5). Day by day, in choice after choice, we follow the example either of Adam and Eve or of Jesus. We insist on our own way or we seek to be in the will of God. When we make a commitment to God, it's never once for all. It's a whole series of decisions. The problem is that we go along with him till our own will is threatened, and then often we rebel.

Our rebellion is often not outright rebellion. We consider it justifiable alternative action. We are sometimes surprised afterwards that we took such a course. Eve was able to to be persuaded that what she was doing was really for her own good. We can think the same. I can persuade myself that the relationship into which I'm slipping, but which I know is unlawful, will really bring me contentment and help me in other ways to live a Christian life. In the Scriptures, the serpent is described as being more crafty than any other creature, and the attacks on God's sovereignty in our lives are often not frontal ones. The devil creeps up from behind.

Sometimes the devil uses our prejudices and preferences, and they become the gods in our lives. They determine what we do or don't do. Somebody's way of talking or his race bothers me, and this becomes an excuse for not helping him. Jesus said to us, "If you greet only your brothers, what are you doing more than others? Do not even pagans do that?" (Matthew 5:27).

Sometimes the devil uses our weaknesses. We let them dominate our lives. We won't do this or that task that we suspect God may be calling us to, because we don't think that is where our strength lies. When Jeremiah was called by God to be a prophet, he wanted to escape from God's will with the excuse, "I do not know how to speak; I am only a child" (Jeremiah 1:6). But excuses of our weaknesses are not valid before God.

Sometimes small illnesses become the controlling factor in a person's life. In suffering, people either let the illness become the dominating factor or they let God be God. St Paul's suffering, his "thorn in the flesh," could have kept him from the missionary work to which God had called him. But he learnt from the lord, "My grace is sufficient for you, for my power is made perfect in weakness" (2 Corinthians 12:9). Paul let God be God in his life.

The challenge to God's authority in our lives is there every day. We can only hope to begin to keep the first commandment if day by day with Jesus we pray, "Thy will be done." It is only as we invite him into our lives and abide in him, that the prayer will be a reality.

O God,
you are the Lord, my God.
How easily I call you Lord,
but so often I want to be
my own Lord.
Help me by your Spirit
to let you be God
in my life,
in every corner of my life.
May Jesus be my pattern,
that I may look for your will
abiding in him.

*2 You shall not make for yourself an idol in the form of
anything in heaven above or on the earth beneath or in the
waters below. You shall not bow down to them or worship them;
for I, the Lord your God, am a jealous God, punishing the
children for the sin of the fathers to the third and fourth genera-
tion of those who hate me, but showing love to thousands who
love me and keep my commandments.*

We like to be in control of situations. When we are dealing with
God, we can't be in control. The appeal of idolatry is that we have
some measure of control. Man made the idol. He was able to
move it about with him. He knew the rituals necessary to pro-
duce rain, to ward off sickness, to ensure a good harvest, etc.
But the reality which is God is always beyond our control by
definition. Our God will not fit into the moulds and patterns that
we try to squeeze him into. J.B. Phillips wrote a book, called *Your
God is too Small*, which talked about the many ways we diminish
God. We don't make physical idols, but we often make God
small, make him fit into our patterns.

There is a wonderful picture in Isaiah 40 in which he points
out the smallness of the gods of idolatry. He writes, "To whom,
then, will you compare God? What image will you compare him
to? As for an idol, a craftsman casts it, and a goldsmith overlays
it with gold and fashions silver chains for it. A man too poor to
present such an offering selects wood that will not rot. He looks
for a skilled craftsman to set up an idol that will not topple. Do
you not know? Have you not heard? Has it not been told you
from the beginning? Have you not understood since the earth
was founded? He sits enthroned above the circle of the earth, and
its people are like grasshoppers. He stretches out the heavens
like a canopy, and spreads them out like a tent to live in. He brings
princes to naught and reduces the rulers of this world to nothing.
No sooner are they planted, no sooner are they sown, no sooner
do they take root in the ground, than he blows on them and they
wither, and a whirlwind sweeps them away like chaff. 'To whom
will you compare me? Or who is my equal?' says the Holy One.
Lift your eyes and look to the heavens: Who created all these?
He who brings out the starry host one by one, and calls them
each by name. Because of his great power and mighty strength,
not one of them is missing" (Isaiah 40:18–26).

Our God is the God who sits enthroned above the circle of the earth, and before him we are like grasshoppers. So our attempts to confine God, to make him small, are always ridiculous. That applies to the words that we use about him. They are always inadequate. He is never fully described or circumscribed by our definition. Archbishop William Temple, in talking of the doctrine of the Trinity, said that the early fathers used the phrase "three Persons in One God" not because it was adequate but in order to avoid saying nothing at all. Any terms in which we think we can hold the infinite God are always inadequate and can even become the thing that obscures God, the way an idol can obscure God. In the Exodus, when Moses was up the mountain, Aaron took the people's jewelry and melted it and moulded it into a golden calf. He then said, "These are your gods, O Israel, who brought you up out of Eygpt" (Exodus 32:4). The idol represented the God who brought them out of Eygpt. But the representation easily becomes the object of worship.

Our aids to worship can also become the end of worship and obscure God from us. Worship can sometimes become an end in itself, rather than opening our hearts and minds to the living God. We want a familiar form of words to be eternal. Some people think that God can speak to them only through one particular translation of the Scriptures. There have been very unholy fights about the words we use for God. Those words make our images of God.

The New Testament talks about a new kind of image of God. In Colossians 1:15, Paul writes of Jesus, "He is the image of the invisible God." Or to the Corinthians, Paul writes about "the light of the gospel of the glory of Christ, who is the image of God" (2 Corinthians 4:4). We have an image, but it is not a graven image. It is a living image, in the face of Jesus Christ. Living images have no definite shape. Although we know the physical shape of a person, the real person is not so easy to tie down. You think you know someone and then are surprised. He has an interest you'd never have guessed. He is placed under stress and you discover that he has inner resources of which you've never dreamed.

Jesus is a living image. Fortunately, we know little of his physical shape. We can't get caught up with that. As a person, Jesus is an elusive image. Here is an image we can never really grasp. His teachings are not easily tied down into a series of simple propositions. You read his words and think you've understood them, but one day you read them again and see something you have never seen before. When we read Jesus' parables, our Lord sets our minds thinking. He opens up our minds to what God might be asking of us, rather than giving a straightforward set of rules. There is always something new springing forth from his word. When Jesus talked about himself, it was in terms that had an openness of meaning. They are phrases that keep expanding. He said, "I am the way, the truth, and the life"; "I am the bread of life"; "I am the resurrection and the life." The image that Jesus presents is always expanding.

If we accept Jesus as the image of God, we will be helped to avoid the pitfall of making God in the image of man. The Bible's teaching is rather that man is made in the image of God. There is more to that infinite God than we can ever hope to comprehend. Every one of us has only just begun to see what it really means to follow him and to worship him.

O God,
I like to have things tied down,
to be able to explain them,
to know what is expected of me.
But you are not a thing,
you are not definable,
you are beyond explanation.
Your call to me is to follow you
and to discover only day by day
what that means.
Help me to look to Jesus,
for he is your living image.
In him I shall be set free
from the idolatry that deceives,
to enter into a living worship
and to walk a living way,
abiding in him.

3 *You shall not misuse the name of the Lord your God, for the Lord will not hold anyone guiltless who misuses his name.*

It's possible to talk about this commandment as though it referred to swearing, but that only touches the surface of its meaning. There were some people in the New Testament who are referred to as "having a form of godlines but denying its power" (2 Timothy 3:5). It is possible to acknowledge the name of God but to take it in vain by denying the reality which lies behind the name. That is why Jesus said, "Not everyone who says to me 'Lord, Lord, will enter the kingdom of heaven, but only he who does the will of my Father who is in heaven" (Matthew 7:21).

We were baptized into the name of the Father and of the Son and of the Holy Spirit. When we fail to live in the power and the calling of our baptism, we take the name in vain. By looking at some of the New Testament references to the name, we can be led to ask ourselves some questions about whether we are taking in vain the name into which we were baptized.

Baptism is a new beginning. Paul explains it: "You were washed, you were sanctified, you were justified in the name of the Lord Jesus Christ and by the Spirit of our God" (1 Corinthians 6:11). Do we live as people who have made a radical new beginning? We take the Lord's name in vain if we fail to accept our justification, the reality that he has forgiven us. Pride sometimes won't allow us to accept the reality that God did something for us that we could never do for ourselves. We do not accept the fact that we are forgiven, and we carry the guilt of sin with us hoping that we can pay for it. Whenever we say, "God can't forgive me for this or that," we take the name of the Lord in vain. In the Lord also we were sanctified — that is, we were made holy. We were declared to be infinitely precious to God. So whenever we despise ourselves or question our value, we take the Lord's name in vain.

Baptism is the acknowledgement that we are children of the Father. John writes, "to those who believed in his name, he gave the right to become children of God" (John 1:12). What does it mean to live as children of God? One clue is in Romans 8, where Paul writes, "You did not receive a spirit that makes you a slave again to fear, but you received the Spirit of sonship. And by him we cry 'Abba, Father,'' (Romans 8:15). We take his name of Father in vain when we fall back into fear. We cannot give way to a fear that no one loves us, for we know that our Father loves us with an overwhelming love. There is no room for a fear that life is controlled by the stars or by meaningless fate. Rather, we live with a new confidence for ''we know that in all things God works for the good of those who love him'' (Romans 8:28).

Since we are children, it means living as members of our new family. So Paul writes, ''Whatever you do, whether in word or deed, do it all in the name of the Lord Jesus'' (Colossians 3:17). Being a baptized person means that the whole of life belongs to God, not just a religious section, and that everything we say or do can be done in the name of the Lord. Whenever by our self-centredness we fail to do that, we take the Lord's name in vain, for we live and work under his name.

Our new family involves family relationships. Jesus prays, ''Holy Father, protect them by the power of your name — the name you gave me — so that they may be one as we are one'' (John 17:11). Living our baptism means recognizing that there is a deeper unity than the bond of simple friendship. When we despise or mistreat other members of the family, we take the Lord's name in vain.

Taking the Lord's name in vain is not merely a personal affair. If we acknowledge him only with our lips, following the form without entering into the reality, we hinder others in coming to know God. Paul wrote, ''As it is written: 'God's name is blasphemed among the Gentiles because of you' '' (Romans 2:24). Our lives and actions are either a witness to the power of Christ, or we give the lie that there is no saving grace in his name.

It is only by a daily vigilance in prayer that we can avoid taking the Lord's name in vain. Paul wrote, ''We constantly pray for you, that our God may count you worthy of his calling, and that by his power he may fulfil every good purpose of yours and every act prompted by your faith. We pray this so that the name of our Lord Jesus may be glorified in you, and you in him, according to the grace of our God and the Lord Jesus Christ'' (2 Thessalonians 1:11–12). By prayer we can know the power of the faith into which we were baptized, so that the name of our Lord may be glorified in us.

O God,
I have been sealed
with your name,
but sometimes I speak and act
as though that seal were
on the surface.
When you marked me
for your own
you washed me,
you made me holy,
you forgave me,
you gave me a new name.
May I not live just by the form of my religion
but by its power.
In my life may I acknowledge
your fatherhood
and my new family.
May I never
take your name in vain
but each day cause your name to be glorified
in Jesus.

---

*4 Remember the Sabbath day by keeping it holy. Six days you
shall labour and do all your work, but the seventh day is a
Sabbath to the Lord your God. On it you shall not do any work,
neither you, nor your son or daughter, nor your manservant or
maidservant, nor your animals, nor the alien within your gates.
For in six days the Lord made the heavens and the earth, the
sea, and all that is in them, but he rested on the seventh day.
Therefore the Lord blessed the Sabbath day and made it holy.*

Society seems to move from one extreme to the other when it
comes to Sabbath observance. Today Sunday is largely ignored.
That may be a reaction to a previous age when Sunday had all

kinds of Sabbath rules and restrictions. Games were banned but uplifting reading was permitted. Older people often have memories of a very negative day. That puritanical Christian Sunday paralleled the Jewish Sabbath of Jesus' day, when the Pharisees had developed a multiplicity of rules as to what you could or could not do. This even led them to accusing Jesus of breaking the Sabbath when he healed the sick. The Sabbath law was very important to them, for after one of Jesus' Sabbath healings they immediately held council against him, how to destroy him.

One of the problems is that the holy day tends to become the end, rather than the vehicle by which we become aware of the reality of God. We do need holy days. We need a structure. Without one day in seven set aside in the community, it is more difficult to have communal worship, for increasing numbers of people are required to work. We need times and hours. We need rules, but the danger always is that they can become ends in themselves. That is what had happened with the Pharisees in Jesus' day. So he says to them, "The Sabbath was made for man, not man for the Sabbath" (Mark 2:27). We are not made to keep the Sabbath but to worship God who has given us the Sabbath to help us come to him.

God knows we need a day of rest. The commandment calls us to do no work, because, as the Lord teaches us through the cyclical pattern of nature, we need periods of rest. Human bodies and minds will not cope with life unless there is a regular structure of rest and renewal. Those who follow our Lord know that it is not merely a matter of not working, but we need a deeper rest in the Lord. We need time to reflect on Scripture and its assurance of his love and purpose for us. If we rest in the Lord, he is a God who renews. In the peace and quiet he gives us new strength to live for him.

We need the Sabbath to reflect on our Creator. In the commandment we are enjoined not to work as an end in itself, and are referred to the Lord's marvel of creation: "For in six days the Lord made the heavens and the earth, the sea and all that is in them, but he rested on the seventh day."

To remember the Creator is to acknowledge that life is meaningful. Among the chaos of the world, the human cruelty, and the natural disasters, we affirm that ultimately there must be a purpose. It is not all accidental. There is a Creator.

To remember the Creator is also to recognize that the Creator has entrusted his creation to us. In a society that so often rapes and pollutes the creation, we need to affirm the responsibility to tend that which God has entrusted to us.

The commandment is a reminder of the Creator's gift to us of time. The New Testament speaks in a number of places about the constraints of time. God has given us a limited time, and we need to redeem the time. Sunday is a day for reflecting on our use of the time entrusted to us. Peter writes, ''The end of all things is near. Therefore be clear-minded and self-controlled so that you can pray. Above all, love each other deeply, because love covers a multitude of sins. Offer hospitality to one another without grumbling. Each one should use whatever gift he has received to serve others, faithfully administering God's grace in its various forms'' (1 Peter 4:7–10). The weekly remembrance of the time God has given us should move us to that renewal of our lives, to the redemption of our time.

Of course, Christians moved the Sabbath to the first day of the week. This was the day which had changed all time, because it was the day of the Lord's resurrection. Time is given a different perspective by the fact that death is not the end of life. Death is a gate in life through which we all must pass. That does not make this earthly life less important, but gives it an even greater significance. Paul finishes his great discourse on death and resurrection by writing, ''Therefore, my dear brothers, stand firm. Let nothing move you. Always give yourselves fully to the work of the Lord, because you know that your labour in the Lord is not in vain'' (1 Corinthians 15:58). What we do today, what we become today, is not meaningless. The significance of our growing today in the love of God and in the fruit of the Spirit is that we shall be at home with the Lord when we pass into the closer presence of our Lord.

Week by week we keep this first day of the week holy, not as an end in itself but to give a new perspective to all time. That perspective includes an awareness of God our Creator and of his purpose in our lives. We are aware of a greater dimension to our life because we see it in the light of eternity.

O God,
it's so easy
to get things
out of perspective.
Nothing is holy in itself
unless it reflects your holiness.
Your holiness is reflected
not in rules strictly observed
but in love.
Give me a new understanding
of the first day of the week,
that it may for me
be a holy day
in which your love is reflected —
your love in creation,
your love in our Lord's death,
your love in his victory over death.
So may your love
grow in me,
to prepare me to meet you
in Jesus.

---

5 Honour your father and your mother, so that you may live long in the land the Lord your God is giving you.

When I was a boy in a small community in England, the doctor held a position of honour. The minister, the policeman, and the postmaster were equally held in honour. The school teacher drank too much, but even he was held in honour because of his position. That kind of honouring is no longer the case. We have passed through the radicalism of the sixties, when structures were thought to be unnecessary. All respect had to be earned, and every person in authority was questioned. The old structures, in family and society at large, were deemed to be constrictive and unnecessary for a new age. Today that shaking up of society is seen as having had some value, but there is also the acknowledgement that society cannot exist with perpetual revolution. Inevitably there have to be authorities.

Society holds together either by respect for authority or by fear of enforced authority. The law is kept either by people having a respect for law and those who enforce it, or by force. Where there is no respect for law, police need to be more and more heavily armed. A government can rule and collect taxes where it has the respect of the people. Other governments rule by the establishment of a police state.

In a family there needs to be honour and respect for parents. Where there is no honour, force comes to be used increasingly. Many families in our society, where the idea of honour for parents has largely vanished, are marked by violence, by wife and child abuse.

There has to be some structure in community, both in the family and in society as a whole. It is a Utopian dream that we can all be equals and that there will be no one in a position of authority over another. Where there have been revolutions and the power of the government or monarchy overthrown, a new elite has quickly emerged. That elite, to keep its position of leadership, has often been forced to become very repressive. We need structures, but we must also recognize that structures often fail because of sin. Sin afflicts both those who govern and those who are governed. Those who are governed push for their own rights over against the community. They each want a little bit more for themselves. They often resent those who govern. Those who govern often spoil the structure by their personal lack of integrity. They seek to feather their own nests, and we are not past the age of patronage. As a government becomes more corrupt, the chances increase that the whole structure will come tumbling down.

In families we see the same breakdown. Children very naturally push for their own way, they clamour for attention, they grow jealous of one another, and they become rude and insolent to parents. Parents lose respect sometimes because of their lack of moral integrity. They have one moral standard for themselves and another for their children. When children see their parents cheat on one another, it is difficult to have a sense of honour. Parents lose respect sometimes because they don't bother with discipline. I have seen four-year-olds talk to their mothers with language which, if they used it to their older brothers, would get them beaten up. The mother that didn't bother to discipline at that point could only expect serious problems when her children become teenagers. On the other hand, sometimes parents lose respect because they are unnecessarily harsh. Sometimes it's because of favouritism. Sometimes it's because they don't work at being parents. The police chief in our community said he noticed that when parents phoned in at 2 or 3 am to report a missing teenager, it meant that the parents had just arrived home and had no idea what their children had been doing for the evening.

Sin on the part of both children and parents spoils families. Where there is no honour for father and mother, families break down. Paul writes about family life in his letter to the Ephesians. After telling children to be obedient to parents, he says, ''Fathers, do not exasperate your children; instead, bring them up in the training and instruction of the Lord'' (Ephesians 6:4). Fathers must not exasperate their children by unreasonableness, by lack of concern, by lack of personal moral integrity, or by acting out of temper. Rather, being a parent means working at training and instruction.

The structure of family life is important. Honour is one of its key elements. There will only be that honour as parents seek faithfully to carry through the role given them by God. But this commandment also applies to the larger family in society. Society will only be healthy as those in authority both are honoured and live such lives of integrity that they are worthy of honour.

O God,
I want my own way.
I see my self to be as good
as the next person,
and so I don't want
to be under anybody's authority;
authority irks me
and I want to be free.

But Jesus put himself under authority —
he was obedient to his parents,
he was obedient to the state,
paid his taxes,
and said, "Give to Caesar what is Caesar's."
That all began because
he was obedient to you.
Help me by your Spirit
to follow him,
to learn a new obedience to you,
so that I may honour
those to whom honour is due
and, in the authority entrusted to me,
I may carry out my duties
faithfully before you
in Jesus.

---

6 You shall not murder.

We watch the newscasts and easily get the impression that in our world life is cheap. The commandment, "You shall not murder," is widely ignored. But that has always been the case. The murder of Abel by Cain is one of the opening stories in the Bible. Man down through the ages has found that the easy way to solve his own problems is to dispose of the other person. The Lord says to Cain, "Why are you angry? Why is your face downcast? If you do what is right, will you not be accepted? But if you do not do what is right, sin is crouching at your door; it desires to have you, but you must master it" (Genesis 4:6-7). Anger has been crouching at our door since the beginning of time. It desires to have us, but in Christ we are called to master it. That is not easy in a society where violence is rampant. On an international scale we spend billions of dollars making weapons of mass destruction. In our cities and towns violence and murder often accompany theft. There is a deep anger that is constantly erupting.

No wonder Jesus says in talking about this commandment, "I tell you that anyone who is angry with his brother will be subject to judgement" (Matthew 5:22). There is a legitimate anger, but Jesus is talking about the abusive anger that goes on and on. Such anger on a continuing basis can destroy someone. You can see this clearly in a child who lives under constant abuse, where the parent takes out his own frustration on the child. The child tends to become withdrawn, and anger is born within him. His personality and his potential for love are murdered. This kind of anger often takes advantage of the structure of the home, the school, the workplace. Someone is given authority and wields it in anger to solve his own problems. The anger we cannot vent on our colleagues or our superiors we vent on those over whom we have charge.

Anger was a problem in the early church. Paul wrote to the Christians in Corinth, "I am afraid that when I come I may not find you as I want you to be . . . I fear that there may be quarreling, jealousy, outbursts of anger, factions, slander, gossip, arrogance, and disorder" (2 Corinthians 12:20). Quarreling, jealousy, and gossip breed anger. There is a similar listing in the letter to the Colossians, with the addition of "filthy language" which so often accompanies anger: "But now you must rid yourselves of all such things as these: anger, rage, malice, slander, and filthy language from your lips" (Colossians 3:8). Anger can destroy the life and work of the church.

It can stop us praying. We read in the letter to Timothy, "I want men everywhere to lift up holy hands in prayer, without anger or disputing" (1 Timothy 2:8). Of course, where there is anger and quarreling, our minds are not seeking the healing will of God.

Anger works against the love of God. If we keep being angry with someone it breeds hatred. John writes about this hatred, "Anyone who claims to be in the light but hates his brother is still in the darkness" (1 John 2:9). As we live with anger and hatred, all our impressions get coloured. We begin not really to see the other person. If someone points out something good about the other person, we can no longer see it. We live in the darkness.

John goes on to write, "This is the message you heard from the beginning: we should love one another. Do not be like Cain, who belonged to the evil one and murdered his brother. And why did he murder him? Because his own actions were evil, and his brother's were righteous . . . Anyone who hates his brother is a murderer, and you know that no murderer has eternal life in him'' (1 John 3:11, 12,15). Death is the condition of the murderer as well as of his victim. Death is the condition of the one who hates, for it erases the image of God.

Anger and hatred lie crouching, waiting for us all. How can we overcome them?

Firstly, since anger when it is fed grows, we need to try to put things right as soon as possible. Paul's advice is, ''Do not let the sun go down while you are still angry, and do not give the devil a foothold'' (Ephesians 4:26–27). Sometimes I hear people quoting another piece of Paul's advice: ''speaking the truth in love'' (Ephesians 4:15). Too often, though, we use that as an excuse to say very bluntly the things we want to say, and we hurt one another. Unless what we are saying is accompanied by loving actions and by prayer, the chances are that we are not speaking the truth in love.

Secondly, we need to try to affirm one another. Some people have problems because they bask in praise and become proud. But that is not the problem of most people. Rather, today, most people need affirmation. Most of us seem to be unsure of our value and of our gifts. We need to be affirmed, to hear a word of encouragement, the word that builds up. If we begin to affirm others more regularly, it will leave less room for anger in us.

Thirdly, we need to recognize that very often the problem lies in us more than in the other person. It is our frustration or our failure or our guilt that breeds the anger. Our need is to recognize this and to come to the Lord for his healing. John wrote, ''This is how God showed his love among us: he sent his one and only Son into the world that we might live through him. This is love: not that we loved God, but that he loved us and sent his Son as an atoning sacrifice for our sins. Dear friends, since God so loved us, we also ought to love one another'' (1 John 4:9–11).

It is as we look at Jesus and become aware of his love to us in our unloveliness that we begin to grow in love. Only his love can overcome the anger that can sap our life.

O God,
anger boils up so quickly
and I'm tempted to nurse it,

to think and think
about my own rightness,
and to be resentful towards
the one who has offended me.
I forget that anger
hurts me
and my friend
and our relationships.
Cherished anger is a killer,
a sign of darkness,
the enemy of the real life
which is marked by your love.
Help me to deal with my anger
by seeking to put things straight
before the end of the day,
by growing as a person
who sees the good and rejoices in it,
and by so looking on the wonder of your love
that I may grow in love
in Jesus.

---

7 You shall not commit adultery.

The Victorian age was portrayed as a sexually repressive period. Some people have questioned whether that is a completely accurate portrayal, but there is no doubt that it was very different from our own day. Today's age will be remembered as a very sexually open time. There is a new openness to discuss the joys and the real problems that centre around sexuality. Unfortunately the openness is not all healthy, for pornography has become a major business. Sex is an open commodity for sale. Often it is pictured as glamour and excitement, as a release from life's problems. The reality underneath is often one of sordid cruelty and broken lives. Public opinion is increasingly aroused concerning the extent of cruelty to women and the exploitation of children.

Many sexual liaisons are casual and outside the bonds of any real commitment. Free love often proves to be very costly, with a sad trail of abortion and venereal disease, a story of broken hearts and broken families. In this world the commandment, "You shall not commit adultery," sounds very old-fashioned and remote. However, it is a necessary guard-rail if marriage is to be what it was meant to be. In the past it has been used as the one test for marriage breakdown in divorce cases. Rightly that is no longer the case. However, adultery often is an outward sign of a breakdown in communication in a marriage.

The commandment against adultery is only a guard-rail. Anyone being married needs more than the guard-rail. There has to be recognition of five things.

First, marriage is a commitment of the will. In the marriage service the response of the bride and groom is not "I do." That is often the response in Hollywood film weddings. In church the response is "I will," because the question is "Will you . . .?" The Prayer Book service has the question, "Wilt thou have this woman to be thy wedded wife . . . Wilt thou love her, comfort her, honour and keep her, in sickness and in health: and, forsaking all other, keep thee only unto her, so long as you both shall live?" The answer is "I will." It is a commitment of the will, for better or for worse, for richer or for poorer, in sickness and in health. If the commitment is only at an emotional level it will not last. The emotions will take over and the way is prepared for seeking comfort outside the marriage in adultery.

Second, marriage is a relationship that reflects the whole person. Marriage is not just a sexual liaison, but one in which two whole persons share their lives. One of the prayers at the wedding service asks "that they may love, honour, and cherish each other, and live together in faithfulness and patience, in wisdom and true godliness." Marriage is a commitment to a relationship that involves every area of two people's lives. That commitment is grounded in a sexual covenant, a commitment in which husband and wife trust themselves to one another. They express the "one flesh" relationship physically, but it is empty unles it is an expression of a commitment to seek in every level of their lives to share with one another and to support one another. Sexual incompatibility is not cured by some physical stimulation, but is often a reflection of many areas of incompatibility. Adultery sometimes seems the answer to a marriage where the sexual activity is lifeless. In reality, adultery is an escape from facing the areas of tension in a relationship.

Third, marriage is a growing relationship. The marriage service is only a beginning. A marriage takes time to grow. People may think they are deeply in love when they get married, but often they look back years later and say, "We didn't really know what love and trust were." Neither partner knows everything about the other on the wedding day. We don't know everything about ourselves, and there are aspects of the other person's character that it takes time to learn. People change over the years, and husband and wife must work through changes together. Marriage is not a static relationship, and adultery often occurs when that is not accepted. A husband or wife could look to another for security rather than facing the realities of change in the marriage partner.

Fourth, marriage does not prevent attraction by another. The temptation to be sexually attracted by another is real. A man who enters into a marriage does not suddenly have blinkers put upon his eyes so that he cannot see anyone else. He can be smitten with blazing attraction. Too often we think that we can stay in control of our emotions, but our human nature is usually weaker than we think. It is rather like riding a bike downhill; for the further you go, the faster you go, and the more difficult it is to stop. A married man who begins to flirt finds suddenly that it has gone a lot further than he intended. The commandment about adultery is meant to be a guard-rail to stop us beginning other relationships. We must always reckon with the strength of sexual urges and the weakness of our self-control.

Fifth, in marriage there is a deeper relationship through Christ. In the marriage service the priest says, "Those whom God hath joined together let no man put asunder." There is the recognition that God has created something new. When two people commit themselves together in marriage, God creates something into which people need to grow. He creates a oneness. There is a parallel to be seen in Paul's understanding of the church. Paul writes to the Christians in Corinth about their sexual problems, their disorder in the eucharist, their greed and selfishness, their quarreling and divisions. He then says to these people, "You are the body of Christ" (1 Corinthians 12:27). God has created something new, and the Christians are to live that reality, they are in all things to "grow up into him who is the head, that is, Christ" (Ephesians 4:15). They are to become that which God has created. It is the same in marriage. God has created a new bonding, and the couple need to grow into that reality. They will do that as they seek God's help, as they receive the grace of forgiveness and apply it day by day. Often they will need to forgive or to apologize, for we so easily hurt the ones whom we love. They will need to pray for each other and for their growth in love. A couple who learn to pray together and to bring their relationship before God daily have the best defence against the breakdown in marriage that so often shows itself in adultery.

There are so many forces in today's world that work against marriage. The seventh commandment is a guard-rail, but is only the minimum standard if a couple is to find the real support that marriage was intended to bring.

Almighty God,
the day I was married
you created a new relationship,
you declared that my wife and I
are one flesh.
But how often I have denied that
by letting my emotions control my actions,
by keeping myself to myself,
by insisting on my own way,
by not sharing my thoughts.
We can only grow in our oneness
by your love changing us,
by the grace of your forgiveness
enabling us to forgive one another,
by the knowledge of your acceptance of us
enabling us to accept one another
as we are
and as we change.

So may we find the marriage
you intended us to have
in Jesus.

---

8 You shall not steal.

Most people would not steal to get it, but they do think that just
a little more money in their bank account would do no harm! We
have a sneaking suspicion that it could bring a little more happiness. If only we could buy that home we had always wanted!
Besides, with money you can get things done. People with wealth
do have the power to "buy" people. There is a feeling of more
security, too, for you can make a provision for old age. No wonder
we would all like that little bit more! The strange thing is that
at all levels of income that little bit more looks attractive.

Money is deceptive. It can bring more happiness, power, and
security, but that is far from guaranteed. Indeed, it can bring
unhappiness. In Luke 18 there is the story of a wealthy young
ruler who was extremely rich but also had a deep discontent. He
realized that something desperately important was missing from
his life, and he came to Jesus asking what he should do to inherit eternal life.

Wealth can buy people, for a little bribe can be effective. Money
can buy friends for the moment, but it does not buy love. The
prodigal son in Luke 15 found that when his inheritance ran out,
so did his new friends. Gert Behanna, wealthy New York heiress,
told her story a few years ago. She had plenty of money, she went
through three husbands, but she found happiness in none of
them. It was only after she had come to faith in Christ, and had
begun to live with people whom she had no desire to buy or
manipulate, that she found happiness.

The sense of security that money can bring is also a false one.
Money has a way of losing its value, and the nest egg that peo-

ple lay up for the future often disappears as they come to meet those retirement expenses. Sickness strikes rich and poor alike. Jesus told of a wealthy farmer who had great plans for the future; "I will tear down my barns and build bigger ones, and there I will store all my grain and my goods. And I'll say to myself, 'You have plenty of good things laid up for many years. Take life easy; eat, drink, and be merry.' But God said to him, 'You fool! This very night your life will be demanded from you. Then who will get what you have prepared for yourself?' " (Luke 12:18-20).

Wealth, rather than bringing happiness and security, can distract us from our true happiness which is to be found in God. We can become overly busy looking after our stocks, keeping our eye on our investments, and improving our property. Jesus tells of the response of people invited to a great feast: "I have just bought a field, and I must go and see it. Please excuse me.' Another said, 'I have just bought five yoke of oxen, and I'm on my way to try them out. Please excuse me' " (Luke 14:18-19). In the parable of the seed which fell in different kinds of soil, Jesus explains about the seed that fell among the thorns: "the worries of this life, the deceitfulness of wealth, and the desires for other things come in and choke the word, making it unfruitful" (Mark 4:19).

Besides keeping us from God, money can keep us from other people. To keep our wealth safe, we need to set up barriers against others who might take it from us. Money often leads to arguments. This is often seen in wills, where some people are excluded and others included in the inheritance. What seem to be harmonious families suddenly divide. There is nothing new about that, for a man from the crowd once called to Jesus, "Teacher, tell my brother to divide the inheritance with me" (Luke 12:13).

There is no security in your wealth. Jesus points to God as the ground of our security. He advises, "Do not worry, saying, 'What shall we eat?' or 'What shall we drink?' or 'What shall we wear?' For the pagans run after all these things, and your heavenly Father knows that you need them" (Matthew 6:31-32). The letter to the Hebrews similarily points us to the providence of God: "Keep your lives free from the love of money, because God has said, 'Never will I leave you; never will I forsake you.' So we say with confidence, 'The Lord is my helper; I will not be afraid. What can men do to me?' " (Hebrews 13:5-6).

In Jesus we have a greater perspective on life. Our anxiety about
tomorrow is placed in the context of a greater tomorrow. We do
not live our lives preparing for retirement, but for our life with
the Lord. St Paul writes, "We know that if the earthly tent we
live in is destroyed, we have a building from God, an eternal
home in heaven, not built by human hands . . . It is God who
has made us for this very purpose and has given us the Spirit
as a deposit, guaranteeing what is to come" (2 Corinthians 5:1, 5).

It is a false estimate of the value of money and possessions that
leads to stealing. We may not steal. We may only cheat on those
little bits of income tax that we explain away: "You can't really
call that stealing." We may fulfil the law, but our calling in Christ
is an honesty that comes from seeing money and possessions in
their right perspective. It is an honesty that values people more
than things. It is an honesty in which a lack of anxiety about things
leaves us free to seek God and his will. It is an honesty in which
we know that we can trust God to give us all we really need. Paul,
at the end of his letter to the Philippians, writes, "My God will
meet all your needs according to his glorious riches in Christ
Jesus. To our God and Father be glory for ever and ever" (Philippians 4:19–20).

O God,
everything around me speaks
of the importance of money.
I think of the things I could get
if I had just a little more money.
I'd then be freer to worship you,
I'd be able to share with others,
I'd have no anxiety about tomorrow.
But you know
that I'm only deceiving myself;
for if I had more
I'd be busier looking after it,
I'd not want to give too much away,
I'd be anxious about devaluation.
Give me a deeper honesty
in which I am aware
that the riches of life are in you,
that you will provide all I need,

that my only security is in you.
May I learn the new values
that are
in Jesus.

---

9 You shall not give false testimony against your neighbour.

Honesty is the key to relationships. Where Paul writes about
speaking the truth, it is in the context of community. He writes,
"Each of you must put off falsehood and speak truthfully to his
neighbour, for we are all members of one body" (Ephesians
4:25-26). Earlier he had explained, "Speaking the truth in love,
we will in all things grow up into him who is the head, that is
Christ. From him the whole body, joined and held together by
every supporting ligament, grows and builds itself up in love"
(Ephesians 4:15-16).

Truth is an integral part of loving relationships. There is no trust
in relationships if there is no truth. If I lie to my wife, it does
something to our relationship. My defences are up in case she
discovers I'm not telling the truth. If she suspects that she cannot trust me, there is strain on her part. Real relationships cannot develop under that strain.

Why do we lie? It is to protect our real identity. We want to
hide ourselves and our actions. We do not want to admit that
we did this or that. So we bring an unreal person to our relationships, and the relationships become unreal. If we lie about another
person, it is often to make us appear better than him. Again, it
is a move to unreality. In my marriage relationship it has to be
the real me, warts and all. My wife does not love me because
I am perfect or am better than other people. She loves *me*, and
it is the same with God. Trying to pull wool over my wife's eyes
usually does not work. It never works with God. If my relationship is to be real, it has to be the real me in it.

Sometimes we are not aware of the seriousness of lying. It does not sound as serious as the behaviour forbidden in the other commandments — murder, stealing, and committing adultery. But lying is associated with two of the most significant events in Scripture: the fall and the passion narrative. In the fall, the devil comes to Eve with lies. "You will not surely die," the serpent said to the woman, "for God knows that when you eat of it your eyes will be opened, and you will be like God" (Genesis 3:4–5). They were both lies and the devil knew it. No wonder Jesus says of the devil, "He is a liar and the father of lies" (John 8:44).

In the passion narrative, Peter lies about his knowledge of the Lord. To the maid and others in the courtyard he swore, "I don't know this man you're talking about" (Mark 14:71). Jesus is condemned by lies at this trial before the Sanhedrin, for "many false witnesses came forward" (Matthew 26:60). When the Jews brought Jesus to Pilate for trial again they lied, "We have found this man subverting our nation. He opposes payment of taxes to Caesar" (Luke 23:2).

Lying can have devastating results. James writes of the smallness of the tongue and of its great power: "Take ships as an example. Although they are so large and are driven by strong winds, they are steered by a very small rudder wherever the pilot wants to go. Likewise the tongue is a small part of the body, but makes great boasts. Consider what a great forest is set on fire by a small spark. The tongue also is a fire, a world of evil among the parts of the body" (James 3:4–6).

But to be "in Christ" is never to be left with just a warning. In him our eyes are turned to the truth. Five associations with truth are made in John's gospel.

First, Jesus comes to us in truth. He is "the one and only Son, who came from the Father, full of grace and truth" (John 1:14). In a very special way the nature of the truth of God is revealed in him, "for the law was given through Moses; grace and truth came through Jesus Christ" (John 1:17). The truth he brings opens our way to God and the life which is in him. Jesus taught, "I am the way and the truth and the life. No one comes to the Father except through me" (John 14:6).

Second, the Spirit that Jesus wants to give us is truth. Three times Jesus describes the Spirit as "the Spirit of truth." "I will ask the Father, and he will give you another Counsellor to be with you forever — the Spirit of truth'' (John 14:16-17). ''When the Counsellor comes, whom I will send to you from the Father, the Spirit of truth who goes out from the Father, he will testify about me'' (John 15:26). ''When he, the Spirit of truth, comes, he will guide you into all truth'' (John 16:13). The Spirit, in contrast to the deceiver, the father of lies, is the Spirit of truth, for God is truth.

Third, it is not surprising that our worship needs to be in truth. In the conversation with the woman of Samaria at the well, Jesus says, ''A time is coming and has now come when the true worshippers will worship the Father in spirit and truth, for they are the kind of worshippers the Father seeks. God is spirit, and his worshippers must worship in spirit and in truth'' (John 4:23-24). Our relationship with God can only be real if there is reality in our approach to him. We cannot come to him pretending to be other than we are.

Fourth, sanctification is always in truth. On the night he was betrayed Jesus prayed for his followers, ''Sanctify them by the truth'' (John 17:17). To be sanctified, to be made holy, is not to have a pious aura, but rather it is to be made real, to be made true. If we are to be real persons, it will be by the sanctifying work of the Spirit of truth.

Fifth, when we are true we are free. Jesus speaks of the freedom found by trusting him. ''To the Jews who had believed him, Jesus said, 'If you hold to my teaching, you are really my disciples. Then you will know the truth, and the truth will set you free''' (John 8:31-32). They did not understand, and expostulated. '' 'We are Abraham's descendants and have never been slaves of anyone. How can you say that we shall be set free?' Jesus replied, 'I tell you the truth, everyone who sins is a slave to sin. Now a slave has no permanent place in the family, but a son belongs to it forever. So if the Son sets you free, you will be free indeed''' (John 8:33-36). If we lie, we become slaves to the lie. We have to live the lie. But the Lord says that when we are able to enter into truth, into reality, there is real freedom.

Any real community is based in truth. Where there is deception, no real community exists, for real community is an interrelationship of real persons. If we are to live in love with one

another, we must live in the truth. The key to honesty with each
other is to be honest before the Lord. He accepts us as we are.
He knows us and no lie ever fools him. If we come to him in truth
and let his Spirit illuminate our minds, we will find that the truth
makes us free. We will be free to grow, because we are honest
about ourselves. That enables us to be free to love and so free
to build real relationships.

O God,
the lie is such an easy device
for dealing with my problems.
It always leaves me a greater problem,
but that's for tomorrow.
So quickly I slip into the falsehood
thinking it will cover me,
but its cover becomes a chain,
forcing me to do the cover-up.
The "white lie" looks as though
it will save my relationship,
but it only pushes it more
into the unreality which cannot last.
Help me to grow in the Spirit of truth
that I may develop deeper honesty
enabling me to admit the real me,
so that I can enter into
real relationships
with my neighbours
and with you.
Then shall I be free
in Jesus.

10 You shall not covet your neighbour's house. You shall not covet your neighbour's wife, or his manservant or maidservant, his ox or donkey, or anything that belongs to your neighbour.

Despite the ups and downs of our economy, we live in a very affluent society. Never have more people had more things. Yet it is also a very discontented society.

Modern technology, along with many blessings, also has a number of curses. One of them is that something new, something apparently better, is always being produced. The record player I bought when I first married quickly became outdated. Then I needed to buy a "hi-fi." Soon my children were advising me that I needed a stereo. Now, if I really want excellent reproduction, I have to face the reality that my present turntable and records are quite inadequate. That is a twenty-five year story! Today, with our computer technology, the rate of progress is constantly speeding up. No wonder we are discontented with what we have, for there is always an improved version available, even though some of the improvements don't fulfil all that is claimed for them.

Our discontent is fed daily by the world of advertising. Millions of dollars are spent to show us that we have needs that we were never aware of. See this happy girl on the beach with a car that has the power and fuel efficiency that come from a turbo that thinks for itself! See this happy family which has attained true contentment because they have discovered a cereal that really crunches! Happy faces and gleaming smiles are produced to show us that other people already have what we ought to have. A commandment about not coveting is really very difficult in such a society.

The commandment is not about general desire. It is about relationship with our neighbours. The tenth commandment is still very important for the health of society and of individuals. This commandment is a constant call for a simple life-style, has important implications for community life, and speaks to man's tendency to try to avoid living in the present.

Firstly, a Christian cannot let his or her life be ruled by advertising. We do not need to buy all that the advertiser needs to sell. If our lives are cluttered with more and more gadgets, we will be increasingly blind about seeing real issues. There is a significant difference between the more efficient corkscrew and the solid gold corkscrew. I need the more efficient corkscrew. The gold one is just another extra item for insurance. A covetous society becomes an indulgent society. An indulgent society has no real concern for the needy.

Christians in the last few years have been seeing that we need to think for ourselves and not have our thinking done for us by the advertisers. It is not easy to define a simpler life-style. Every individual and family need to face what that means for them. A computer in one home can serve a purpose and enable some tasks to be done more efficiently. A computer bought because everybody ought to have a computer these days can become just another encumbrance that collects dust. A wardrobe that has to be changed constantly by the dictates of fashion can make us so clothes-conscious that we let dress become far too dominating a factor in our acceptance of people. There are no easy answers to what we should or should not have. Rather, we need to think twice about whether we need to buy something. We need to examine how we spend our money and what place possessions have in our lives. If we are always wanting something else, always coveting what others have, we need to ask God to give us wisdom and grace.

Secondly, we should be aware that coveting destroys community. The commandment is not just about personal desire. It is about relationship with our neighbours. It is about a jealousy of our neighbour, about wanting what he has. If we constantly hanker for our neighbour's possessions, it destroys any real community with him, for our eyes become fixed on the possessions rather than on the neighbour himself. A relationship based on desire can never seek a neighbour's good. Whenever possessions become more important than people, community is in danger.

Thirdly, coveting can lead to unreality, to a state in which we are always saying, "Well, if only I had . . . I would be happy." This means that we never enjoy the present. To covet is never to live in the realities of the present moment. The "if only" syndrome is the mark of a dream world. It is characterized not only by "If only I had this or that thing," but shows itself in other ways. We are discontented with our work, and become convinced that all would be different if only we had another job that some-

one else has. We become discontented with the place in which
we live, and rather than seeking to make a contribution to it, we
spend our time wishing that we lived somewhere else.

There is a two-fold remedy for the "if only" syndrome. The
first part is to affirm daily that our lives are in God's hands. We
commit ourselves to God and believe that he can direct our lives.
He has something for us to do in every situation. Our happiness
is not in what we possess, the position we hold, or the place we
live, but in God. If our goal in life is in him, we shall be able to
say with St Paul, "I know what it is to be in need, and I know
what it is to have plenty. I have learned the secret of being content in any and every situation, whether well fed or hungry,
whether living in plenty or in want" (Philippians 4:12). The secret
of Paul's contentment was his faith in the indwelling Christ, for
he wrote, "I can do everything through him who gives me
strength" (Philippians 4:13).

The second remedy is to develop the habit of giving thanks.
If we regularly make time to give thanks to God, it will grow and
smother our complacency and coveting. In visiting the sick, I have
been deeply moved to hear someone say, "Bishop, I am so
thankful." Then they have gone on to tell me of the things for
which they were thankful, rather than to relate all their pains and
difficulties. It was a genuine thankfulness that put their needs
into perspective.

We should not forget to be thankful, because at the heart of
our worship is the eucharist. That title comes from the Greek
word "to give thanks." This service is a thanksgiving that God
in the richness of his mercy has given us everything in Christ
Jesus. In regularly giving thanks, we will accept the fact that our
life, our situation, is in God's hands, and we will learn to say
with St Paul, "Oh, the depth of the riches of the wisdom and
knowledge of God! How unsearchable his judgments, and his
paths beyond tracing out! Who has known the mind of the Lord,
or who has been his counsellor? Who has ever given to God, that
God should repay him? For from him and through him and to
him are all things. To him be the glory forever. Amen" (Romans
11:33–36).

O God,
how easily I look at my friend
and see his car or his computer,
wishing that they were mine.
The wish grows larger in my mind,
and my friend grows smaller in my affections.
My discontent hides from me
your goodness and the reality
of your many blessings.
Give me a thankful heart;
help me to count my blessings
and to name them one by one.
Only then shall I get things in perspective,
seeing my friend larger than his possessions
and being able to think straight,
so that I may develop a life-style
which has the simplicity that is real
in Jesus.